Critical Guides to French Texts

86 Beaumarchais: Le Barbier de Séville

Critical Guides to French Texts

EDITED BY ROGER LITTLE, WOLFGANG VAN EMDEN,
DAVID WILLIAMS

BEAUMARCHAIS

Le Barbier
de Séville

John Dunkley

Senior Lecturer in French
University of Aberdeen

Grant & Cutler Ltd

1991

© Grant & Cutler Ltd
1991
ISBN 0-7293-0331-4

I.S.B.N. 84-401-2065-6

DEPÓSITO LEGAL: V. 1.552 - 1991

Printed in Spain by
Artes Gráficas Soler, S. A., Valencia

for

GRANT & CUTLER LTD
55-57, GREAT MARLBOROUGH STREET, LONDON W1V 2AY

Acknowledgements

I am indebted to the Carnegie Trust for the Universities of Scotland for a research grant which enabled me to visit Paris to consult relevant material in national collections there, and to the University of Aberdeen, which allowed me study leave for this purpose.

I should like to register my gratitude to Professor Robert Niklaus for suggesting that I should undertake the writing of this book, to Madame Jacqueline Razgonnikoff, of the Comédie Française Archives, for the information and documentation which she put at my disposal, to Dr Philip Robinson, of the University of Kent at Canterbury, for his kindness in making available to me the results of his researches into the music of Beaumarchais's plays, as well as to my wife, Eileen, for her help with the proof-reading.

Contents

Introduction 9

1. Evolution of *Le Barbier* 11

2. Characterization: Methods and Process 18

3. Dramatic Structures 55

4. Language and Music 71

5. Farce, Mimicry and Philosophy 81

Select Bibliography 91

Introduction

T H E four-act version of *Le Barbier de Séville* was first performed at the Comédie Française on 26 February 1775 and, by
31 December 1990, it had received 1,198 performances there. It
was performed for the first time before the French court on 14
March 1775, and roughly once a year thereafter until 1788.

The exclusive focus of this study is the play itself, and limita-
tions of space prevent the exploration of ancillary material.
Chronologies of Beaumarchais can be found in several editions
of his plays, and a number of good biographies are available
for those wishing to study the writer's life in greater detail.
The *Lettre modérée* is also largely ancillary in that it replies,
with a degree of disingenuousness, to the *Journal de Bouillon*'s
criticism of the five-act version of *Le Barbier,* which was
performed only once. The two *Compliments de clôture* are
interesting, if marginal, adjuncts to the play, since, although
they may never have been staged, they are strongly reminiscent of the *parade* genre, which crosses that of *Le Barbier de
Séville* at one point in its development. It is, moreover, because
the chequered origins of *Le Barbier* have left visible traces in
the final version that I have included an introductory chapter
on the play's development. In the subsequent chapters I have
tried to discuss those elements which most clearly contribute
to the impact of the play. Some of the conclusions are my own;
for others, I am indebted to the many previous scholars who
have written about Beaumarchais's plays.

A list of the editions of *Le Barbier de Séville* currently
available in bookshops is included in the bibliography. The
Pléiade, Garnier, Blackwell, Livre de Poche and Folio editions
are all worth consulting for the critical material they contain.
The present study is based on the Bordas edition because it

contains useful secondary material, has line numberings and is likely to remain in print for a long time. References, other than footnotes, consist of the italicized number ascribed to a work in the bibliography, followed, where necessary, by an indication of a relevant chapter or pages.

1

Evolution of *Le Barbier*

T H E definitive, four-act version of the play is the end product of an unusually chequered process of composition. Until as recently as the 1960s, it had been generally believed that the play originated in a lost *parade* supposedly written by Beaumarchais for performance at the house of the financier Le Normand d'Etioles (1717-99), the husband from whom Madame de Pompadour separated when she became Louis XV's mistress. *Parades* were short, farcical plays which had originated as entertainments performed outside the theatres at fairs to attract the public to come in and watch something more substantial. They traditionally adopted characters from Italian comedy, Cassandre, Isabelle, Colombine, Léandre, Gilles and Arlequin. The upper classes, who also frequented the fairs, 'adopted' the genre around 1730, and *parades,* composed by lesser known authors who stooped to the occasion, were privately performed in the houses of wealthy amateurs, where aristocrats often played alongside professional actors. Although in 1768 this moonlighting was specifically forbidden to the actors of the Comédie Française, the opportunity for frequenting the aristocracy on a transitory footing of intimacy and for earning extra money provided an inducement to flout the ruling. The plot-structure most frequently, though by no means exclusively used was that of the hero, 'le beau Léandre', winning the hand of the heroine, Isabelle, despite the opposition of her father, 'le bonhomme Cassandre'. The details of the lovers' machinations naturally vary considerably, as does the way in which the servants, Arlequin and Gilles, contribute to the action. The situations which *parades* presented were often scabrous, and they traditionally incorporated obscene and pseudo-plebeian Parisian language with abusive *liaisons*

(known as *cuirs*) for the amusement of the spectators. Pierre
Larthomas (*22*, pp. 28-29) notes the chief linguistic characteristics of Beaumarchais's own *parades*: the accumulation of
linguistic errors, malapropism, the absurd or striking confla-
tion of two words or conventional expressions, modified pro-
verbs, tautology and cacophony. To the best of our knowledge,
Beaumarchais was the author of (strictly speaking) four *parades* between 1760 and 1772. Though they are cruder in
tone than anything the Comédie Française of the time would
have accepted, Beaumarchais's *parades* do not descend to
the level of tastelessness which marks some examples of the
genre.

The idea that *Le Barbier* started life as a *parade* was first
advanced by the nineteenth-century critic Eugène Lintilhac
and was repeated in a number of later studies. Indeed the
similarity of situations and comic devices present in *Le Barbier* and the works to which Lintilhac alluded, especially Fa-
touville's *La Précaution inutile,* lent the idea plausibility. But
in fact, Lintilhac's theory was elaborated on the basis of association of ideas and implication, and the one notably absent
ingredient was proof. E. J. Arnould, in a seminal article published in *French Studies* in 1962 *(12),* pointed out the extreme
fragility of Lintilhac's 'éloquent tour de passe-passe' and re-
gretted the currency it had achieved. He reiterated his view in
the edition of the play which he published in the following
year *(1),* and his *Genèse du 'Barbier de Séville'* which appeared
in 1965 *(13).* In this later work Arnould drew for the first time,
in a modern, scholarly and systematic way, on the Beaumarchais family archives and on extant manuscripts, and, by
printing together all the stages in the evolution of the play
which were known at the time, revealed clearly the modifications which the text underwent in the years 1772 to 1775,
between the first extant manuscript and the work as we know
it today. At that point, then, the *parade* theory appeared defin-
itively laid to rest, and the origins of *Le Barbier,* prior to the
stage at which Beaumarchais turned it into an *opéra comique,*
of which no full text survives, buried in obscurity.

Arnould also printed, *inter alia,* a number of fragments drawn from the Beaumarchais family archives which seemed of interest though of little scholarly value, except for their obvious thematic connection with *Le Barbier* (*13,* pp. 105-13). Arnould remained unaware of their full significance, which became apparent nine years later with the publication of René Pomeau's article '*Le Barbier de Séville:* de l'"intermède" à la comédie' in the *Revue d'Histoire littéraire de la France (24).*

It was in the same issue of the *RHLF* that the descendant of the author, Jean-Pierre de Beaumarchais, published for the first time an incomplete sketch *(un intermède)* entitled *Le Sacristain (14).* The existence of this text in the family archives had been generally known since 1966, when it had figured in a Beaumarchais exhibition at the Bibliothèque Nationale. So many similarities to *Le Barbier* did the extant (first) part of *Le Sacristain* prove to have, that it was clear that the original idea of *Le Barbier* was to be located there. The basic text of *Le Sacristain,* when taken without its variants, bears no resemblance to a *parade. Le Barbier,* then, started life not as a *parade* but as an *intermède.*

This *intermède,* modelled on the Spanish *entremeses,* which Beaumarchais had come to know during his stay in Spain in 1764, was composed in the following year on his return from Madrid. It uses the stock Spanish comic figure of the lustful churchwarden as the disguise which the hero, Lindor, employs in his attempt to gain access to Pauline, the wife whom the aged and impotent Bartholo keeps in seclusion at home. Lindor comes to the house claiming to be a music master for Pauline, sent by Dom Bazile, the organist at the convent of Monseigneur Saint Antoine, to replace him during his illness. Allowing for the brevity of the text of *Le Sacristain* as we have it – the latter part is not extant – the similarities of structure and detail between it and *Le Barbier* are clear. As well as characters with similar functions and several instances of precisely replicated wording, both plays contain a bogus drunken soldier, a billeting warrant episode and a Bartholo who says things twice.

A study of the autograph manuscript and related documents reveals the successive stages in the development of the text of *Le Barbier*, and it is now established that a *parade* was one of the stages in its evolution. The original *intermède*, when reworked as a *parade*, ended with Bartholo being drubbed by the lovers' friends disguised as ghosts and it was performed at Etioles along with *Jean-Bête*, itself a *parade*, which was composed sometime between 1765 and late 1772. Manuscript material reveals additions to the original *Sacristain* text of both a scurrilous kind, which would turn it towards a *parade*, and of a musical kind, which would turn it into an *opéra comique*. It is unlikely that Beaumarchais would have taken the trouble to modify *Le Sacristain* with no purpose in mind, or to make such modifications to the text of a work intended only for the Théâtre Français, since they would have served only to make it *less* acceptable there.

The only typical features of *parades* to remain notably absent from the addenda which made the *Sacristain* into a *parade* are linguistic ones; slang and false liaisons are not included. But this can be explained by the fact that specifically low-Parisian deformations of the language would have been inappropriate in a *parade* set in Spain and in which the characters were not plebeian.

The interest of the question of whether the *parade* really does represent one stage in *Le Barbier*'s evolution is not a purely antiquarian one. Its value for a study of *Le Barbier* is that it has left traces in the final form of the play where a sexually charged atmosphere prevails, and it also accounts for the fundamental ambiguity in the character of Rosine and Almaviva's shift from dissolute would-be seducer to devoted and honourable suitor.

So much for the *parade;* let us now turn to the *opéra comique,* which is the first work to bear the title of *Le Barbier de Séville* and to include the name of Figaro.[1] The change of

---

[1] I retain the French 'opéra comique' since to translate the term would lead to ambiguity. In the late eighteenth century it equates to 'comédie mêlée d'ariettes' and implies spoken dialogue intermingled with words set to well-known airs (see the *New Oxford Companion to Music,* edited by D. Arnold [Oxford, O.U.P., 1983] article 'Opéra comique', by John Warrack, vol. II, p. 1320).

title is the necessary concomitant of further changes in the plot. Lindor is no longer, as he had been in *Le Sacristain,* the seducer of the impotent Bartholo's wife, but has become Le Comte, the aspirant to the hand of Bartholo's ward, now named Rosine. It is not therefore on the humiliation and punishment of an inadequate and tyrannical husband that the ending needs to focus. The outcome of the action is to be the marriage of the young lovers, and the indecent, *parade*-style themes of impotence, adultery and cuckoldry are no longer at issue. The 'ennobling' of Lindor into Le Comte made it necessary to free him of some of the material concerns involved in courting Rosine, and, clearly, a capable factotum was the ideal type of character to assume this function. By giving this task to Figaro, Beaumarchais moves the Count more towards the margins of the action, and the resourceful and organizing servant comes to occupy the centre of the stage. (For fuller details of these developments, see *14, 24* and *26.*)

As a talented and enthusiastic amateur musician, Beaumarchais wanted, according to his friend and biographer Gudin de la Brenellerie, to see more extensive use made of music in the theatre and had accordingly incorporated couplets in his *Barbier de Séville,* mostly set to Italian or Spanish tunes with which he had become familiar during his stay in Madrid. He offered his *opéra comique* to the Théâtre Italien as the theatre most likely to produce this kind of work. But the Italiens turned it down, for reasons which the author's friends were able to explain to him. J.-B. Guinard, known as Clairval (1735-95), was the leader of their chorus of counter-tenors and very influential in the actors' committee which accepted or rejected works submitted for production. Clairval was the son of a wig-maker and had for a time followed the same profession before he joined the Italiens. Naturally enough, he was reluctant to do anything in his new career which might remind the public too obviously of his previous one. As a result of its rejection by the Italiens, Beaumarchais set about remodelling *Le Barbier* to make it acceptable to the Français. By all accounts the *comité de lecture* was delighted with the work. Its acceptance for performance is noted in the *Registres* for 3 January 1773, and the manuscript received the approbation of the censor Marin on 12 February.[2] Rehearsals began within one month of the play's acceptance, and the first performance was scheduled for the Shrove Tuesday following. But after his scandalous brawl with the unstable Duc de Chaulnes over a disputed mistress, Beaumarchais found himself in the For l'Evêque prison (a prison specially used for actors who misbehaved; it was demolished in 1783) between 24 February and 8 May, and the performance was postponed.

Rehearsals were resumed on 5 February 1774, and the censor Arthaud approved the text on the same day. Though the play was due to be performed on 12 February, orders were issued on the 11th for the cancellation of the first night, much to the disappointment of the public, which had received the author's witty *Mémoires sur l'affaire Goëzman* with enormous interest. The cancellation of the performance was probably prompted by the *lieutenant de police* d'Argenson, who had been attacked in the *Mémoires,* and by Madame Du Barry, who wanted to thwart the wish of the dauphine, Marie-Antoinette, to see the play.

At the end of the same month came the personal disaster when Beaumarchais lost his civil rights (he was *blâmé*) by the judgement which the Parlement Maupeou issued at the end of the Goëzman affair (26 February 1774).[3] Having spent the remainder of the year engaged in diplomatic missions in an attempt to get his civil rights restored (a proceeding typical both of Beaumarchais and of the Ancien Régime), he again requested permission, in December 1774, to go ahead with preparations for the performance of the play. A version in five acts was finally staged on Thursday 23 February 1775, and it was a total flop. Beaumarchais had injected into the original four-act text far more digressions and reflections derived from his personal experiences of the previous four years,

---

[2] Three different censors were eventually to examine the play, and different manuscripts were submitted on each occasion. Full details about the manuscripts and editions of the text can be found in *13,* pp. 116-22.

[3] Goëzman was a *conseiller* in the unpopular reformed *Parlement* which Maupeou instituted to replace those of Paris, Douai and Rouen in February 1771. The former regime was restored in August 1774.

and more insipid witticisms and plain irrelevancies, than the simple plot could bear (see *1*, p. xix, n. 25). What is more, this recently expanded version of the text (see *12*, p. 345) was not the one which the actors had got used to in rehearsals, and their performance may consequently have lacked polish.

The remedy was obvious, and Beaumarchais and the actors adopted it. For the second performance, on Sunday 26 February, they went back to the four-act version, and the result was a resounding success.

The printed text of the play by itself appeared for the first time on 30 May under Ruault's imprint; this (*pace* Arnould) is, properly speaking, the original edition. A second edition of the play was published at the end of July, again by Ruault, and with it the first edition of the *Lettre modérée*.

2

Characterization: Methods and Process

I N order to understand how Beaumarchais builds the characters of the *Barbier* and why they make on us the impact they do, it is important first to understand what the author meant by *un caractère*. This will go some way towards explaining how he managed to take the hackneyed and very simple *précaution inutile* theme and create around it a work more dynamic and more memorable than many of the other plays whose theme was the same.

It would be pointless to look to Beaumarchais to provide 'characters' in the sense that Molière and some of his immediate successors did before *comédies de caractère* declined in the early eighteenth century. The *comédies de caractère* of the late-seventeenth and early-eighteenth centuries offered protagonists with a dominant character trait which coloured the rest of their personality and conditioned and explained their reactions to the world around them. With Beaumarchais, who set out to revive the comic genre in a modernized form, the case is different.

His ideal conception of the theatrical protagonist would be to translate on to the stage the kind of person which he saw himself as being, and, with Figaro at least, he succeeds. His idea of a dramatic character is an individual with an outlook or personality of which different, possibly even contradictory, elements are brought to the fore in differing degrees by his contact with others and by the pressures of the situations which he and his fellows create and need to react to. In broad terms, this implies an unremitting tension between the impulsions of the individual character and the total situation which confronts him. One element of this situation, more prevalent in Beaumarchais's *drames* than in *Le Barbier,* is what the author calls *la disconvenance sociale,* whereby the character has personal attributes seemingly out of keeping with the position in which he finds himself. This can be taken in two ways: either the character's general position in the world is not in keeping with his personal attributes or, on a more mundane level, the character finds himself in a particular and transitory situation which mismatches these attributes. Figaro, with his resourcefulness and versatility, may well have visible affinities with the low-born picaro, but his intelligence and ability to organise and manipulate people and events seems to be worth more in terms of moral dynamism than would be suggested by the subservient or undistinguished roles which, we are told, he has performed before the play opens.

The 'character', then, taken in Beaumarchais's sense, is marked out by his will-power, by his vigour and by the energy he puts into his activities – activities whose ethical value can cover the whole range from commendable to disreputable. The Figaro of *Le Barbier* is both instrumental in rescuing Rosine from Bartholo and at the same time acts virtually as a procurer to the Count. Above all, he is quickly adaptable to changes going on around him, and is therefore himself a focus of change, a being in perpetual movement, far removed from the stability of the characters of classical and immediately post-classical comedy. Since it is continual evolution that marks the character's existence, that existence largely eludes simple definition. Beaumarchais's personal philosophy of life as evidenced by his varied occupations and by the energy and determination with which he pursued them, is one whereby character is affirmed and perpetually re-created by constantly coping with situations and striving to affirm one's mastery over Chance. Adversity is countered by an alert intelligence and a constant, optimistic re-routing of the critical path towards the fulfilment of one's projects.

It has been suggested (*17,* p. 31) that, of all Beaumarchais's characters, only Figaro, whom biographers frequently place in parallel with his creator, comes anywhere near this ideal, and that even he, especially but not exclusively in the later *Mariage de Figaro,* is at times thwarted by Chance, or expends a great deal of energy to no better purpose than placing an apposite quip or impressing the gallery with his panache. The fact remains, though, that chance setbacks and wasted energy do not actually detract from the dynamism of the character. What they possibly do detract from, however, is depth or solidity of character. Coping with events individually as they arise, sometimes winning, sometimes losing to Fortune, but constantly regrouping one's forces for another skirmish with life's difficulties, can come very close to being the plaything of Chance, which one can defeat in individual encounters but over which one knows that no final victory ever comes. 'Le hasard a mieux fait que nous tous... Ainsi va le monde', wrote Beaumarchais in *Le Mariage* (IV, 1). The temptation, and it may be one to which Figaro finally succumbs, is to mask the real anguish of that situation with a cheerful and superficial insouciance, witness his well-known remark: 'Je me presse de rire de tout, de peur d'être obligé d'en pleurer' (*Le Barbier,* I, 2). But even here one can only say 'may be', since the admission of nonchalance is couched in a quip, and could be put there more for its wit than its truth, and certainly, it would not be the only doubtful claim that Figaro makes about his own character.

Le Barbier and *Le Mariage* are often referred to as 'the Figaro comedies', and Figaro is one of those dramatic characters, like Tartuffe and Lady Macbeth, whom everyone has heard of. This notoriety is partly due to the 'attraction' of the much stronger impression he makes in *Le Mariage*. Indeed, an examination of the structure of *Le Barbier* reveals that Figaro is on stage less than the other principal characters. It is his almost continuous presence on stage in act I, and his having the title-role in both *Le Barbier* and *Le Mariage* that are chiefly responsible for creating the impression that his part is larger than it really is. In addition, once the play is under way, an audience tends, when Figaro is offstage, to assume that he is actively engaged behind the scenes in furthering the desired outcome of the plot. This is the effect of a powerful dramatic character, and clearly, in the construction of any character, the opening scenes are crucial.

When we first see Figaro, it is early in the morning. (In two of the manuscripts, Beaumarchais had specified 9 a.m., but seems finally to have settled on a rather earlier time of day.) The streets are deserted, except for the Count, who has just explained (in a rather blunt expository monologue) his ulterior motive for haunting the shadows in front of Bartholo's house. Enters a jaunty figure, a *majo,* brightly and fashionably dressed and carrying a guitar. He offers a strong visual contrast to the semi-darkness and the Count's sombre disguise, and he is in the process of composing a song. The immediate impression he makes is of someone lively. He dresses brightly and rises early for no specific reason, and the inference is that here is someone keen to get on with the business of living life to the full. And his singing gives the impression that he is carefree. The words of his song promptly reinforce our immediate impression: he sings of his love of wine and idleness. What he later tells the Count about the full life he has led since leaving his service, plus the versatility he will later show in the course of the action, will belie the words of the song on which part of our first impression is based. But, as spectators, we will retain the impression without noticing the contradiction, since the continuous advance of a play, especially one which moves as rapidly as this, militates against simultaneous analysis.

Another important point is that he appears to be revealing his innermost self through his song, not in what he says – which he admits is literary artifice – but by letting us see him in the act of composition. We are made to witness the apparently private thoughts and feelings of the character. We see that he is pleased with the results of his efforts as a song-writer, and we also see his private doubts about the correct use of vocabulary, and hence infer that he has a degree of self-awareness, and takes a pride in doing well in the eyes of other people. He is intelligent enough to make a judgement of the operatic fashions of his day (ll. 34-35) and to express it in the first of the maxims which will punctuate much of what he says later in the play. And he shows that he is cynical enough and versatile enough to operate the mechanism by which a commonplace statement can be dressed up to look like a subtle thought (ll. 39-50). Finally, we learn from his reference to 'messieurs de la cabale' that, like his creator, he is familiar with theatrical life, and this impression will be amplified and refined in what he later tells the Count.

What is important here is the amount of information Beaumarchais manages to put across to the audience in so short a space, both visually and verbally, and the careful method by which that information is orchestrated to predispose the audience to view Figaro in a particular way. Moreover, the character is made to create this impression, alone, *before* we see him interacting with anyone else.

His first encounter with another character begins at line 59, when he and the Count notice each other, and the importance of this part of the scene for the characterization of Figaro is that the impression of openness which the spectator received, when he was allowed to 'spy' on Figaro earlier in the scene, can be sustained in the conversation with Almaviva, because it is cast as a meeting of two long-standing and genuine *friends*. Their relationship is made to look like one of equals, with *tu* and *vous* reduced to a mere convention. It becomes clear at once that Figaro is independent, and not an employee, and indeed the Count will soon be asking, as a favour, for Figaro's help in what is initially presented as a rake's escapade, thus emphasizing the intimacy and durability of a friendship which has survived a longish period of separation.

The initial exchanges between Figaro and Almaviva (ll. 60-73) are interesting chiefly for linguistic reasons, but they serve, on the level of characterization, to make their intimacy plain at the outset, and this is underlined by the exclusively masculine use of the jocular insult (*maraud,* etc.). One would instinctively expect that the ages of Figaro and Almaviva would be more or less the same, and yet Préville, who first played the part of Figaro, was over fifty in 1775, and an understudy needed to stand in for him from time to time when he was prevented from performing by his attacks of gout. In modern times, however, the tendency has been to cast in this role someone more comparable in age to Almaviva. If, as we learn later (ll. 727-28), Figaro has a small daughter (who naturally does not figure in the *Mariage*) one would expect him to be in his early thirties, since male commoners married on average at around twenty-eight during the seventeenth and

eighteenth centuries. Aristocratic men of the highest rank generally married earlier, at around twenty-one.[4]

When Almaviva explains his difficulty in immediately recognizing Figaro ('Te voilà si gros et si gras', ll. 69-70), we are
reminded of Figaro's apparent prosperity, his aura of well-
being – not necessarily obesity – and Figaro's contradiction of
Almaviva's impression ('C'est la misère', l. 71) is used as a
witty springboard for a full account of Figaro's activities since
he left the Count's service. It is important to bear in mind that,
from the encounter with Almaviva onwards, what Figaro tells
us about himself is intended not just to inform the audience
but is also to be assimilated by another character. Beaumarchais has therefore to make its content and presentation con-
form to the parameters of their relationship as they were laid
down in lines 60-70. The information can therefore be taken
as 'accurate', within the terms of the play, but we expect,
rightly, that its nature and presentation will be lighthearted
and that Figaro's professional failures will be glossed over,
while the emphasis will be placed on the resilience which uses
them as stimuli to new endeavours.

Almaviva's recommendation of Figaro to the minister
(ll. 81-82) underlines the fact that they parted on good terms
(Figaro later alludes again to his *protections,* this time from an
unspecified source, at line 1401), and when the Count later
recalls that Figaro had been 'un assez mauvais sujet', while
still retaining his master's goodwill, we may conclude that
Beaumarchais is implying that it is a certain roguishness that
recommends them to one another. An eye to profit (a trait
commonly associated with servants in comedies) rather than
strict conscientiousness has marked Figaro's career as a vet on
a stud farm, and it squares perfectly with the relationship of
Figaro and the Count as we have seen it unfold so far that, of
all the possible details of this job, it is the malpractice it entailed
that Figaro singles out to tell Almaviva, presumably because
this is the type of activity which he knows from experience

---

[4] See F. Lebrun, *La Vie conjugale sous l'ancien régime,* Paris, A. Colin,
1975, pp. 31-33.

will amuse the Count. Contemporary audiences would also
have found the malpractice funny, since it is suggested that
conventionally amusing regional groups (Galicians, Catalans
and Auvergnats) thrived on horse medicine – but clearly this
point is only very tenuously linked to the process of characterizing Figaro.

As the conversation proceeds, Figaro recounts how his
passion for literary and musical composition (a preoccupation
shared by nearly all the characters) has lost him his official
post. Some critics have seen in this and the references to
calumny in the play a reflection of Beaumarchais's own experience with the Parlement Maupeou. An autobiographical
allusion has also been seen in the remark that the pretext for
removing Figaro from his post had been that literary pursuits
were incompatible with business activities. Beaumarchais may
have felt that his dramatic ventures, his musical activities and
his social life encouraged people not to take him seriously in
financial, diplomatic or legal fields, but to me the point seems
debatable. Allusions to the author's own experiences may be
discernible in these lines (94-96, 99-105) as they are in others,
but one should avoid pursuing this line of argument too far,
since it illuminates the characterization of Figaro only in a
limited way. It indicates to us, as it no doubt did to a cross-
section of Beaumarchais's contemporaries, that the author
could see the dramatic potential of events in his own life, and
the possibility of getting even with enemies by holding them
up to public ridicule or scorn. But material from an autobiographical source is not in itself a necessarily useful element in
the structuring of a dramatic character. It may indeed be pos-
itively detrimental to the drama, as the failure of the five-act
version proved, possibly because, unlike other material, its
dramatic effectiveness is not the primary reason for its inclusion.

A further point needs to be made about this stage in the
Figaro-Almaviva conversation: its artificiality. We have clearly been drawn into a fantasy world from the very beginning of
the play. This particular conversation is primarily a part of
the exposition, telling us what Figaro is like and what his
history is. It is in fact a hybrid, an amalgam of lifelike ex-

changes, such as the ellipsis of line 106 (a frequent feature of conversation between people familiar with one another's ways of thinking and speaking) and of literary elements, which serve to characterize Figaro, and his creator, very well, like the alexandrine of line 96 and the aphorisms of lines 107-08, 111-12 and 114-16. A conversation with an interlocutor who larded his contributions with quotations and maxims would, in the real world, be quite intolerable. But to the spectator, who accepts that he is watching a fantasy, it comes across as a conversation between two newly reunited friends, in which Figaro *appears* to tell his news with such spontaneity that we do not get the impression of witnessing an exposition scene at all. In this respect scene 2 stands in marked contrast to scene 1.

Having told Almaviva about his misfortunes as a dramatic author, Figaro is prompted to explain what made him leave Madrid. In a splendidly – and, we now feel, typically – exuberant single sentence covering nineteen lines, he explains how his disenchantment with his existence as an author has prompted him to lead the picaresque life, finally to become a barber in Seville. Two significant points in the characterization of Figaro emerge from these lines. Firstly, the literary figure of the picaro had just such an optimistic resilience in the face of misfortune as Figaro is showing here, and the literate portion of the audience may well, consciously or otherwise, have subsumed Figaro into the picaro category in their own minds and associated him with its general characteristics. (Though it is clearly unwise to generalize about the cultural levels of audiences from the past, a number of spectators would probably have been put in mind of Lesage's *Gil Blas*.) In this case, Beaumarchais would be linking Figaro to a well-established tradition, with the consequence that the social and moral connotations of the character are broadened, and the need for detailed exposition reduced. Secondly, through a pun, we learn for the first time that Figaro is now practising as a barber. The hero of the Spanish *entremés* was traditionally a barber who, unlike Figaro in this play, was never seen to shave his clients on stage. Figaro is, then, the object of a double link with Spain, through the picaro and through the *entremés*.

The unfolding of Figaro's character continues in scene 4, after the introduction of Bartholo and Rosine (sc. 3). One scholar, Navarri (*23*, p. 137), saw lines 225-28 as an element of cynicism in the character. But, while Figaro is openly recognizing that it is in his general interest to retain the goodwill of an influential friend like Almaviva (and will indeed reiterate the thought in line 398), to call this cynicism may be an overstatement. Recent researches in social history have shown that the basis of the master-servant relationship evolved during the eighteenth century away from one founded on the provision of material and (supposedly) moral welfare in exchange for loyal service, towards one whereby efficient service was exchanged for cash payments. Beaumarchais may be reflecting this newer trend in the way he makes Figaro conceptualize his relationship with the Count at this point. This is only one strand in Figaro's way of looking at the relationship, of course, and a minor one, if one bears in mind the much stronger emphasis constantly placed on the friendship of the two characters. Figaro certainly voices no objection to serving the Count; good-natured and tolerant irony is his way of viewing social inequality and Almaviva's mild exploitation of him, judging by lines 273-76. Technically, it is a fact too that Figaro is not a servant, but an ex-servant now working independently, and Scherer quite rightly points out the significance of the suppression of an episode in the closing scenes of *Le Barbier* in which Figaro was offered a financial reward and refused it because it would vilify him (*30*, p. 216; *13*, pp. 404, 405). Nevertheless, there has been a tendency among critics to lay less stress on Figaro's technical independence than on the *literary* lineage which predisposes a spectator unconsciously to subsume him into the 'comic servant' category, albeit with important differences from the general run of such characters (*31*, pp. 123-25; *29*, pp. 293-95; *4*, pp. 22-23).

In the course of his examination of the role of Figaro, Descotes considers the character in *Le Barbier* within the context of the Figaro 'trilogy'. He argues that, with Figaro's use of the traditional methods of secret notes, disguises and drugs for overcoming a traditional adversary *(le barbon)*, his role is not markedly dissimilar to that of the Crispins and

Scapins of other comedies. In the two succeeding plays, his adversaries and his methods are quite different. 'Le véritable rôle de Figaro, dans le *Barbier*', Descotes concludes, 'est exclusivement celui du valet d'intrigue. Lui conférer une plus large ampleur, c'est jouer par avance un personnage différent' (*19*, p. 106). This is a pertinent and accurate observation about the best way of interpreting the part. But it would be a mistake to underestimate Figaro's originality and the extent to which he is divorced from the traditional comic servant. Jean Emelina rightly indicates that Figaro has none of the usual shortcomings of comic servants (idleness, drunkenness, gluttony, cowardice, etc.) which gave moral validation to their masters' social superiority, but comes across as an *individual* (*20*, p. 296).

And, as we saw earlier, he is the only character in this play to qualify as a *caractère* in the sense in which Beaumarchais understands the term. The remainder of act I, scene 4 adds another notable element to the characterization of Figaro. His quick thinking has already been shown by his ready wit; now, to complement that information, we are shown how this gift is to be turned to practical ends. While the Count is fondly wishing that he could remove everyone standing in the way of a possible meeting (or should one say 'tryst'?) with Rosine (ll. 281, 283), Figaro is already assessing the practicalities of the enterprise, which he has thought of *before* the Count voices his wish, and hit upon the expedient of using drugs. He is also aware of the need for acting quickly. The speed of his calculations is such that the Count is visibly unable to follow his pace and is left alternating between puzzlement and admiration. And so, of course, is the spectator, just as Beaumarchais no doubt intended he should be.

Essentially, Beaumarchais has created Figaro by the end of act I, scene 4, and subsequent details will generally complement what we already know, rather than extend it. But I, 6 adds a significant detail to the characterization process: Figaro's showmanship, which is especially in evidence in lines 400-04. If the Count and the audience are puzzled as to what exactly Figaro plans to do in Bartholo's house, Beaumarchais increases our amusement by having Figaro present himself as an omnipotent magician – a particularly suitable persona to place in this fantasy context. Both with the context and with the character, Beaumarchais is playing on the balance between our rationality and our imagination. Figaro's optimism and resilience and the tones of realistic camaraderie with the Count are made to contribute to our rational perception of the character as a remarkably lively human being, while his incredible versatility, his aphorisms, his unshakable confidence in his quasi-magical power to overcome obstacles – and indeed the very fact that he should be involved in Bartholo's household at all – promote the vision of a fantasy character, strongly reminiscent of the fairy-godmother of children's literature. [5]

Whereas Figaro, whether present or absent, dominates the play, it is Almaviva that we meet first. The opening scene of the play indicates what is going on and introduces the character whose interests are central to the plot. The first thing we learn about him is that he is acting and appearing out of character, as he will do increasingly by assuming the disguises which Figaro invents for him. Noble, rich, handsome, sated with libertine pleasures and disillusioned with social and sexual relationships among his own kind, he has left the court circles of Madrid to come to Seville, a city symbolizing provincial 'natural' values, in contrast to the 'civilized' ones prevailing in the capital. [6] Thus we find him, dressed in a dull,

[5] The characterization of Figaro as a magician has also been noted by S. and J. Dauvin (*18,* p. 41), who stress the importance of words in the context of magic: 'Pour Figaro, pas de limite à la *puissance créatrice des mots*: il lui suffit d'exprimer son projet pour que celui-ci semble déjà réalisé: en deux mots, le chirurgien s'est fait Merlin, sa lancette est devenue "baguette" (I, 6)'. And they note how this impression is carried on into the subsequent action, when L'Eveillé begins to ache all over simply as a result of hearing Figaro speak (II, 6) and when Bartholo begins to talk in an (uncharacteristically) confused way (III, 14), once Figaro has pronounced him *fou* (III, 13). The Dauvins' observation is a perfectly plausible reading of the textual evidence, and one which, I think, is perhaps more in harmony with the general tenor of the play than the more pedestrian (but still viable) explanations for the same events, according to which L'Eveillé is simply a suggestible dullard, and Bartholo is havering because he is in a rage.

[6] Seville's reputation in eighteenth-century France appears to have been good. Jaucourt's article in the *Encyclopédie* (XV, pp. 132b-137a) is full of praise for the beauty of its churches, its fertile surroundings and its lively trade. Only its university and its slave-market attracted Jaucourt's disapproval.

ecclesiastical disguise, sighing lovelorn beneath the casement of an inaccessible beauty in the hope of catching a glimpse of her.

The stock situation and the character are both intended to look familiar and, if not totally impossible, at least highly improbable. But the formula of the court aristocrat acting atypically is calculated to arouse our interest. He tells the audience himself that he is doing something unusual, quaint and slightly laughable ('[un] aimable de la cour... me prendrait pour un Espagnol du temps d'Isabelle') in seeking for sincere, disinterested love rather than the kind on offer at court. (Contemporary audiences tended to be more sensitive than we are today to the sentimental appeal of 'natural', as opposed to 'civilized' behaviour.) Once our curiosity has been aroused by the statement of the Count's reasons for being where he is, the monologue *has* to come to an end. Had it been prolonged, it would have turned dull, because it presents a basically amusing situation in tones of some seriousness. As a means of conveying information it is effective, but as a method of characterization it is unsubtle. It also needs to be borne in mind that, for contemporaries but not for us, the setting and the situation of this opening scene are strongly reminiscent of a number of *parades,* with the balcony overhanging the street and the 'beau Léandre' figure, and that, while it is useful for Beaumarchais to be able to use the stock situation as a frame of reference to enable audiences to identify broadly the type of character they have before them, he must avoid overemphasizing Almaviva's links with Léandre if he wants to develop the present character and play along rather more original lines.

Ostensibly the second scene of act I serves to characterize Figaro more than Almaviva, whose contribution to the conversation consists mostly in asking questions about Figaro's activities since their separation. But although the Count does not offer the kind of developed, personal view of life we get from Figaro, the process of his characterization moves forward. The sincerity in human relationships which we learnt, from I, 1, that Almaviva prizes is illustrated by the opening exchanges between himself and Figaro. The friendly tones of the dialogue show that the Count is amiable and (like Rosine) free of aristocratic pretentiousness, and this is only possible because he is absolutely at ease in the social hierarchy – a point which Beaumarchais will underline throughout the play. Time and separation have not weakened the temperamental harmony which underpinned the former relationship of Figaro and the Count. They can still understand one another *à demi mot*, and the Count does not hesitate to tease Figaro in fraternal tones about his involvement with medicine, his literary pursuits and his wayward character. Figaro's reactions to being teased are significant; he does not let the points go unanswered, but the answers he gives are light-hearted and witty. By implication, then, the Count is further characterized as the sort of person to appreciate reactions like these in which humour and assertiveness blend together. Although the Count has in fact started off their conversation by using Figaro as an adjunct to his ecclesiastical disguise, this fact is rapidly overlaid by the exchanges which follow, and throughout the scene the Count's genuine interest in Figaro (he asks questions) is doubled by his obvious pleasure in conversing with a close friend. By using his ample characterization of Figaro to elicit from the Count reactions which indicate to the spectator a temperamental harmony which transcends social boundaries, Beaumarchais is characterizing the Count in the most economical way possible.

The interdependence of Figaro and the Count has been noted by several critics (see especially *25*, p. 149) and they can be construed as forming a composite 'hero-figure' to which the commoner Figaro contributes his intelligence, experience, energy and stamina, and the aristocratic Count his natural accomplishments (musical composition, play-acting), his polish, his influence, his wealth and his social prestige. (Beaumarchais's idealized self-image may be discernible here.)

The events of the third scene, in which Rosine drops her song and message from the casement, are crucial for the characterization of the Count since, when we meet him again in scene 4, he will be reacting to Rosine's first unequivocal sign of interest and discussing with Figaro a situation in which he has the highest degree of emotional involvement. But the opening lines of the scene (ll. 209-21) are not entirely straightforward, for the Count's first and third speeches contain an element of parody: '... examinons cette chanson dans laquelle un mystère est sûrement renfermé. C'est un billet!' (ll. 209-10), 'Ma chère Rosine!' (l. 221). At this point Beaumarchais is colluding intellectually with the audience as it smiles at the Count's overplaying of the role of enraptured lover. The passing of clandestine messages and a lover's enthusiasm were such wellworn dramatic commonplaces that it is not surprising that Beaumarchais distances himself from them in this way. It is interesting from an aesthetic point of view to note that the Count's 'enforced' self-parody is cast around the other parody in which Figaro mimics Rosine's counterfeit distress over dropping her song.

Once Figaro has drawn the obvious conclusion from the Count's behaviour ('vous faites ici l'amour en perspective', l. 223), the Count briefly explains the background to his present situation (ll. 229-34). Captivated by Rosine's beauty when he saw her at the Prado, then a promenade for people of fashion, he has initiated inquiries about her all over Madrid. As an aristocrat he has the necessary means of doing this, but the way he has gone about it is in marked contrast to the much lower profile he has so far adopted in Seville. We shall discover later that his typically aristocratic methods, relying on the unreliable discretion of others, attracted the notice of Bartholo. The methods he will use under Figaro's direction will not, of course, be any more subtle.

The Count's inquiries have brought him information which contains an important error: he believes that Rosine is Bartholo's wife. Although he claims to prize emotional sincerity (I, 1), he shows himself (like the traditional Léandre) undaunted by the prospect of adultery and of the consequent cuckolding of the bourgeois Bartholo, a point which contemporary critics noticed. A residue from the earlier versions of *Le Barbier,* this 'problem' is soon resolved. The Count's intended immorality is not translated into action, since Figaro immediately dispels his error about Rosine's marital status – news which Almaviva receives with a predictable outburst of enthusiasm for sweeping Rosine out of Bartholo's clutches. The Count's reaction, which includes the words 'il n'y a pas un moment à perdre' (ll. 242-43), has the dual function of suggesting an element of youthful hot-headedness and of marking an acceleration of the action.

The remainder of act I, scene 4 is partly devoted to the characterization of Bartholo, amplifying information which we gleaned from his appearance in I, 3, and it partly serves to further our knowledge of the Count. The new urgency he sees in his situation makes his remarks more clipped than before, and twice the stage directions describe him as appearing *impatienté* – comically eager to get things moving, and it is at this point that he discovers the real usefulness of Figaro to his enterprise.

As we noted earlier, Beaumarchais makes Figaro do all the planning at this stage (ll. 281-300) in order to introduce Almaviva into Bartholo's house, and the Count's only contribution is to use his influence with his friend the colonel of the Royal-Infant regiment to obtain a fraudulent billeting warrant – a farcical device, and incidentally, a social comment too: noble birth may be a matter of chance, but it brings very real benefits. As far as characterization is concerned, the Count's role in all this simply proves that he is less resourceful than Figaro. Under Figaro's direction, he is, however, shown to have a certain talent for acting (hence we have a play within a play) and can assume the disguise of a tipsy soldier without much difficulty. French literature habitually depicted Spanish aristocrats as being very aware of their dignity, and this view is in evidence in the *dénouement* of *Le Barbier*. Such a view is not, however, inconsistent with the Count's clownish involvement in this escapade. This is partly because, in the context of a fantasy like this one, these socially realistic considerations are less generally applicable, and partly because acting, for many *French* aristocrats, would not be out of character at all. Indeed when *Le Mariage* was performed at court, members of the royal family figured in the cast.

In act I, scene 6, the Count shows a talent for musical improvization, which Figaro admires. The two lines of Rosine's sung reply to the Count's song and the resolution he makes a few lines later ('Lindor... je dois l'aimer constamment', ll. 380-81, and 'je suis à ma Rosine... pour la vie', l. 393) add the last necessary element to the basis of the plot, and with this the characterization of Figaro and Almaviva is effectively complete. Despite the presence of conventional elements in the composition of both characters – especially of the Count – the process by which they are developed is a subtle and economical one, and they are well placed in a setting where the realistic and the plainly fantastic mix easily together. Figaro is the more original and interesting creation, and the Count, being cast very much as a foil to him, comes across as a slightly paler figure.

By the end of act I, we have been introduced to all the main characters, but whereas the spectator has a complete picture of Figaro and Almaviva, Bartholo and Rosine have as yet only been outlined. So far, we have seen Bartholo and Rosine once (I, 3) and Bartholo alone once (I, 5) and, with the exception of Rosine's messages to the Count, neither has yet communicated with either of the other principal characters. Rosine has *seen* the Count loitering in the street outside the house in the mornings but, at the point when we first meet them, has only a tenuous hope of being befriended (or delivered) by someone about whom, given her seclusion, she knows nothing. Bartholo is already under pressure to marry her as soon as he can. Though, when he composed act I, scene 3, Beaumarchais planned to have Bartholo be suspicious of any man who might come into contact with Rosine and be aware of the Count's inquiries in Madrid, the audience watching the play does not acquire this information until Bartholo's later conversation with Bazile (II, 8). However, even without offering the full reasons for Bartholo's virtual incarceration of Rosine in act I, Beaumarchais makes Bartholo's actions in regard to her seem coherent. This is partly the consequence of the historical precedents for the role and partly because of the way he shows Bartholo airing his prejudices in the first few lines he speaks.

Both the tone and the content of Bartholo's very first exchanges with Rosine are intended to convey the traditionally antipathetic personality of the *barbon*. His first terse question (l. 171) is in marked contrast to Rosine's obvious pleasure at breathing the fresh air through the open window, and we are immediately put in mind of a prison superintended by an inquisitor – a stuffy inquisitor, moreover, whose capital ignorance of the *précaution inutile* theme will be his Achilles' heel. His attitude to life is encapsulated in a few lines (ll. 179-85): an authoritarian who loathes all the things which symbolize the progress achieved by the Enlightenment in every domain, intellectual, scientific, theological, medical, philosophical and even... theatrical. A pervasive antipathy to modernity colours Bartholo's attitude to his profession, and this will later be amplified in act II, scene 13, when he defends it with comic hyperbole against the impertinences of 'Lindor l'Ecolier'. Their exchanges appear to have been conceived more for the author's pleasure in airing a series of well-worn jibes than for the particular purpose of characterizing Bartholo, but his professional pride comes across nonetheless. When the medical profession had been satirized by Molière and his successors, it had been as charlatans who hid their incompetence behind a façade of obscurantist language. Bartholo, however, is not in fact portrayed as a professional obscurantist or a pedant. To the audiences of the 1770s, his contempt for inoculation and quinine would suggest that his medical science was old-fashioned. His diagnosis of Rosine's faint (II, 15) – which, for the purpose of the plot, Beaumarchais does not let him see through – is redolent of out-dated, though not at that period entirely discarded theories. Medically, Bartholo is an anachronism and he has more affinities with the grotesque reservists of Death from the seventeenth century than with the doctors of most eighteenth-century comedies, who were generally urbane and reassuring with their patients, especially with women.

Bartholo's attitude to the past and the present is well summarized by G. Bonneville, who writes: 'dans tous les domaines... Bartholo est, à la lettre, un réactionnaire. Vous remarquerez qu'il ne s'agit nullement d'un attachement sentimental au passé: Bartholo n'aime pas le passé, il déteste le présent. Il n'a pas le goût des vieilles choses: sa haine est concertée autant que dépourvue de poésie' (*2*, p. 69). The only reference Bartholo ever makes to the past comes in act III, scenes 4 and 5, when he is shown recalling, and adapting to the occasion, a song from his youth, and it comes across as a mixture of inanity and bad taste.

When Rosine drops her song into the street, Bartholo cannot avoid going down to search for it, since it would be inappropriate to let Rosine go and too time-consuming (and possibly embarrassing) to send a servant. But Rosine's stratagem is very unsubtle, and Bartholo obviously sees through it (ll. 200-02) – a point confirmed by his monologue in act I, scene 5. Beaumarchais is careful, in deriving the basic theatrical character of Bartholo from the *Docteur* (Baloardo) of the *commedia dell'arte* and the Cassandre of the *parades* to differentiate him at the outset from these stock figures by making him, as he said, 'un peu moins sot que tous ceux que l'on trompe au théâtre' (*Lettre modérée* ll. 275-76). His intelligence, which becomes increasingly obvious as the play unfolds, makes him what Scherer has called an *obstacle résistant*. Outmanœuvring Bartholo will take all the quick thinking his opponents can manage, plus a certain amount of authorial contrivance. Just as we are constantly *shown* Bartholo's intractability, we are *told* of it too, with the Count's words: 'Que ce diable d'homme est rude à manier!' (III, 3).

As well as the information we can glean from Bartholo's own words and actions we have Figaro's well-known description of him in I, 4: 'C'est un beau, gros, court, jeune vieillard, gris pommelé, rusé, rasé, blasé, qui guette, et furette, et gronde, et geint tout à la fois' (ll. 248-50). This description, which is a condensed version of a much longer one (see *13*, p. 169), is well-known not for what it tells us about Bartholo, but rather for what it tells us about Beaumarchais's use of words, and I shall return to it in that context later. This is not to say, though, that it is uninformative. The literal meanings of some of the words are eclipsed by the overall impression created by the sentence as a whole. (Something similar is the case with the Count's *signalement* of Bartholo in II, 13, where the impertinent words are reinforced by the connotations of the music.) The impression created in the spectator's mind may well be one of a small, fast-moving rodent.

Figaro's next two descriptions of Bartholo are more purely factual: 'brutal, avare, amoureux et jaloux à l'excès de sa pupille, qui le hait à la mort' (ll. 252-53), and: '[Il a de probité] tout juste autant qu'il en faut pour n'être point pendu' (l. 257). Though he is said to be *avare*, he is clearly no latterday Harpagon; after all, Figaro owes him three years' rent, and Bartholo himself snaps at Bazile for being exclusively preoccupied with money (ll. 1889-90). His *avarice* consists in getting hold of what he can while paying out as little as he can get away with. It is well summarized in two sentences: (Bartholo) 'Je me soucie bien de l'argent, moi! A la bonne heure, je le garde' (ll. 1890-91) and: (Bazile to Bartholo) '...vous avez lésiné sur les frais' (l. 655).

By the end of the first act, we have enough information about Bartholo to be able to predict the tenor of his subsequent behaviour. The construction of the character is generally consistent throughout the play except in the handful of instances where Beaumarchais needs him to commit particular mistakes in order to allow specific developments of the plot (i.e. where characterization is sacrificed to structure). Beaumarchais's method consists in delineating firmly the basics of the character as early as possible in the play, and thereafter amplifying them and making one or two plausible additions. Thus Bartholo's reference to conformism and his reliance on authority (l. 179) and his authoritarian treatment of Rosine in I, 3 foreshadow the bullying of his servants in II, 7 (ll. 593-99). While his behaviour with them appears dictatorial, it could be argued that he has a right to act firmly with his servants, although *that* degree of firmness would, in 1775, mark out a master as being behind the times by the best part of a century. When Figaro uses the word *brutal* (l. 252) he is giving us one of the keys to Bartholo's character, and it is illustrated by the sarcasm and inquisitorial tones he adopts whenever he is questioning someone whom he takes to be in a weaker position than he is. Though more subtly translated, Bartholo's attitude to Rosine over the dropping of her song (II, 4, ll. 530-41), her ink-stained finger and the missing paper (II, 11) is basically the same as his attitude to his servants. His *brutalité* takes the attenuated form of aggressive self-confidence in the following scene (II, 12) when he goes on to confront an apparently drunken soldier, dismissing Rosine with the words: 'Je ne suis pas timide' (l. 763), and when he tries, politely but firmly, to show the Count the door in the final scene of the play. He is finally defeated more by authorial intervention and legal realities (the marriage of Almaviva and Rosine and the need to avoid provoking an investigation into his maladministration of Rosine's property) than by being actually outwitted.

One of the words which figured in Figaro's initial description of him was *rusé,* and this characteristic – a novelty in the *barbon* – is upheld throughout the play. Perpetually suspicious and capable of seeing through the stratagems of his opponents (though not their disguises), Bartholo is seemingly perfectly lucid about the quality of his attachment to Rosine. We are prepared for the existence of a one-sided attachment between guardian and ward, not only because this conforms to the theatrical tradition, but also because Bartholo has been passing Rosine off as his wife since their arrival in Seville. Figaro had, as we have seen, described their relationship in lines 252-53: 'amoureux et jaloux à l'excès de sa pupille, qui le hait à la mort'. But, in fact, Bartholo reveals himself as distinctly more *jaloux* than *amoureux.* The rare occasions when he speaks gently to Rosine (III, 4 and IV, 3) are the signs not of affection but of manipulation and duplicity. It is his remark at the end of IV, 3, 'A la fin, je la tiens', that reflects his real feelings towards her. More than anything else, he is possessive, and this obstinate desire to possess her is ruthlessly self-indulgent: 'Il vaut mieux qu'elle pleure de m'avoir, que moi je meure de ne l'avoir pas' (IV, 1, ll. 1617-18). As Bonneville aptly puts it: 'C'est un égoïsme d'autant plus ignoble qu'il est lucide' (*2,* p. 135). This attitude stands in strong contrast to all the many Enlightenment texts which stress the value of *friendship* as the basis for family relationships.

If Bartholo seeks to possess Rosine, he leaves little doubt about his motive, which amounts to little more than lust. He makes at least three references to it (II, 15, l. 1023; III, 5, the song; IV, 3, l. 1705), and he is clearly shown to lack the sensitivity which would make him realize the likely effect of such innuendoes on Rosine. For her part, she does make one remark which might be taken as indicating her doubts about his capacities when she says to him (II, 15, ll. 1021-22): 'Si

vous pouviez me plaire...' – not, be it noted, 'si vous *saviez'*.
This interpretation is supported by Bartholo's immediate reply.[7] Pomeau is severe but perfectly accurate when he writes
of Bartholo: 'Il est "blasé", et s'il s'acharne à posséder Rosine,
c'est moins amour que convoitise. Cette "jolie petite mignonne"
agace son appétit; il lui chante, égrillard: ...la nuit, dans
l'ombre, / Je vaux encor mon prix! L'âge l'a durci et desséché.
Il a de l'intelligence, de l'activité (il "toupille"), mais peu de
cœur. Son désir, dépouillé de toute sentimentalité, tourne en
une jalousie maniaque, vite odieuse' (*25*, p. 153).

The logical conclusion to what I have said so far about
Bartholo is that the character is repulsive. Descotes realized that
the role could lend itself to such an interpretation (*19*, p. 67) and
he also pointed out that Bartholo's undoing at the end of the
play stems from his refinement of malevolence in trying to
ensure that the Count is not only thwarted in love but dishon-
oured and imprisoned too. In his unpleasantness Bartholo is
reminiscent of the villain figure in some *drames* and *mélo-
drames,* and, of course, Beaumarchais's inclination, if not his
talents, led him to write *drames.* But comedies can have villains too, the only necessity being that we, as an audience,
must never be allowed to imagine that they will win the day.
In comedy if not in life the guardian/father figure is habitually
thwarted. What reassures us in the present instance is partly
that tradition and partly the fact that, for all Bartholo's intelligence and ruthlessness, we cannot take the character seriously,
and this results from the way Beaumarchais presents him.

One key to an understanding of why Bartholo is funny
seems to lie in an idea which Bergson formulated in *Le Rire.*
Why is it funny, he asked, when an orator sneezes at the
most pathetic moment in his speech? The general answer he
evolved was that: 'Est comique tout incident qui appelle notre

---

[7] These allusions to lust and impotence illustrate the origins of *Le Barbier*
as outlined in Chapter I. Rosine's remark is an adaptation of a note which
appears in Beaumarchais's *Notes et réflexions* (*7*, p. 31): '"Aimez-moi, je vous
prie", disait un amant dédaigné... "J'y consens, dit la dame, mais plaisez-
moi".'

attention sur le physique d'une personne alors que le moral est en cause'.[8] And this is precisely the case with Bartholo. If he were just an intellect, he would be sinister, but the physical side of him is very obviously present, constantly recalled and constantly undermining the intellectual side of him. There is a certain unseemly urgency in his allusions to his virility. When he tries, before the eyes of the audience, to equal the younger generation on its own terms, the result is absurd singing and ungainly dancing, and when he sits down his real age catches up with him and, all exhaustion and aching legs, he dozes off (III, 4). His body, then, does not live up to the ambitions of his ego, and rather goes its own way. As if that were not enough, it requires ongoing maintenance. In Bartholo's case this means shaving, carried out in a public room – with a lack of taste which Rosine observes. Moreover, it is, in a sense, the body that finally defeats Bartholo, since it is his physical absence that allows the marriage of the Count and Rosine to take place. In Bartholo's case, then, the physical body, and especially its shortcomings, are constantly emphasized and work to neutralize the more sinister impact of his intellect.

While he does not emphasize the physicality of Bartholo, Descotes rightly points out that much of the humour of the part stems from the words the character uses, though I am not sure that the example he gives (*19*, pp. 69-70) – the interrogation of Rosine in II, 11 – is the best one, since it seems to lend itself more easily to a threatening interpretation by the actor playing the part. A more obvious example might be Bartholo's habit of saying the same thing twice.

Descotes makes another important point when he says that Bartholo's part is comic when set against those of the other characters because 'il est le repoussoir' (*19*, p. 69). Beaumarchais disparaged the use of contrasting characters as a technique of characterization, seeing it as *petit, peu vrai* and fit only for use in a *comédie gaie,* as if this genre required less skilful characterization than more serious ones. Yet our experience of drama teaches us clearly that to set characters in contrast

---

[8] H. Bergson, *Le Rire,* 273rd edition, Paris, Presses Universitaires de France, 1969; p. 39.

is a common technique because it is generally very effective. Indeed, it is difficult to see how it could be avoided in cases where the central issue is a conflict of interests and when, as here, the conflict is polarized between age and youth, confinement and freedom, revulsion and attraction, etc. Coulet was right to point out that, whatever he claimed to believe, Beaumarchais had recourse to this technique in practice (*17*, p. 26).

Of the four principal characters Rosine is the most ambiguous. Like the others she will later appear in *Le Mariage* and, like Almaviva and Figaro, she will also figure in *La Mère coupable.* In her case especially, it has to be borne in mind that the subsequent developments of the character are not ones which Beaumarchais had fully thought through when he was composing *Le Barbier,* and that they are irrelevant to our perception of the Rosine who appears in this play. It is not her dramatic future that needs to be taken into account, but her dramatic past. Her derivation from the Pauline of *Le Sacristain* still shows through the character whom Beaumarchais claims to be trying to portray as a *charmante enfant* (*Lettre modérée, 2,* l. 490).

As the focus of interest for the other three major characters, Rosine is talked about from the very beginning of the play. From the first scene we see the extent of the Count's infatuation with her and gather that her daily appearances at the casement fuel his devotion. Nothing is said which would serve to characterize her during the first two scenes, and, as with Figaro and the Count, her first appearance on stage gives us our first knowledge about her.

Her very first words, 'comme le grand air fait plaisir à respirer', typify the character as we shall come to know her. She is shown as appreciating things *natural,* she is attracted to refined, sensual pleasure (music, the open air), and savours a feeling of freedom which contrasts sharply with the conditions under which she is normally kept. Her opening sentences – which do not lend themselves to rapid delivery – provide a tonal contrast to the terse question from Bartholo which comes immediately after. Before she drops her song, an argument develops between her and Bartholo. We gather that they probably argue often ('Vous injuriez *toujours...*') and that she is

aware of the intellectual developments of the Enlightenment
(Bartholo's list would make no sense to an ignorant interlocutor) and approves of them ('*notre* pauvre siècle'). The fact of
arguing with her guardian and her support for things he dislikes
denote a degree of assertiveness.

Then she drops her song and calls on her skulking suitor to
pick it up. I referred to this move earlier as 'unsubtle'. Indeed,
it is; even Agnès in *L'Ecole des femmes* thought of basically
the same tactic, and she was characterized as being far less
sophisticated than Rosine. Bartholo is not fooled by the ploy
but, for the reasons indicated earlier, has to go along with it.
The moment after he gives up the obviously pointless search
and goes back into the house, Rosine speaks of her plight:
'Mon excuse est dans mon malheur...' (ll. 203-05). Ostensibly
directed to the Count and Figaro, these words are particularly
important as information for the audience. They are her personal commentary on her situation and, in keeping with the
value she sets on symbols of freedom, express her loathing for
Bartholo and his tutelage. It is the injustice of her situation that
she offers as her *excuse* for dropping a note to a man whom
she does not know. What she does is an act of blatant impropriety, and Beaumarchais cannot let it pass without a justification unless he is prepared for audiences to form an initial
impression of Rosine as a brazen girl whom it is only prudent
to keep in (theoretically) strict confinement. The presence of
this justification implies that the author definitely does not
want us to see Rosine in that light. He later referred to her as
a *charmante enfant,* but the *Lettre* is a *post hoc* commentary,
in parts frankly disingenuous, and in any case charm and
youth do not necessarily imply innocence.

In scene 4, Almaviva reads Rosine's note aloud, and the
puzzle for the audience increases. Is the note a sign of the
candour of an *ingénue,* or of the alacrity of a coquette in taking
the initiative? Is the tragic *infortunée* a term to be taken at
face-value, or is it an authorial parody of a damsel in distress?
Is dropping a note the last resort of a desperate prisoner, or
the first impulse of a flirt? The fact of dropping the note is in
a way more important than its contents, since the questions it
asks are pointless. Almaviva is not obliged to reveal his real

name – indeed, he doesn't – and no gallant would reply that
his intentions were other than honourable, whether it was true
or not. In fact, Almaviva's intentions at this point are *not*
honourable, since he still believes that Rosine is married. And
even when he finds out that she is not (l. 241), he still lies
about his intentions, pretending to be content to adore her
from a distance (ll. 370-74), while really planning an elope-
ment (ll. 243-44). Figaro's reaction to Rosine's note (ll. 217-20)
echoes the audience's problem, but does nothing to resolve it.
That such an important question mark should hang over one
of the main characters may suggest a flaw in Beaumarchais's
technique of characterization. It is, on the other hand, arguable
that what Figaro expresses as a mixture of *adresse* and *ingé-
nuité* simply mirrors the complexity of real people, and there
is just about a strong enough element of reality in all these
characters to allow such an interpretation.

Rosine reappears in scene 6 and sings two lines pledging
her love for 'Lindor'. Figaro rightly concludes that she is
'hooked' (*prise*), and the Count reiterates his intention of making her his wife. If *Le Barbier* were any less of a fantasy, one
would straight away conclude that Rosine was possibly a flirt
and certainly a fool, and that Almaviva was no better. Real
marriages of inclination could, after all, hardly be based on
such tenuous acquaintance.

It is Rosine who opens act II with one of the five monologues which Beaumarchais gives her in the play. Rosine's
monologues can mostly be seen as summaries of the situation
and expressions of her anxiety when she has no one on hand to
confide in, and they contrast with Bartholo's, which are largely outbursts of irritation. Beaumarchais uses Rosine's thinking
aloud at this point in a number of different ways. It reminds
the audience of the sympathy between herself and Figaro, and
of his intention of incapacitating the servants; it emphasizes
Rosine's longing for freedom and sense of oppression, and
above all it underlines her inexperience, since she commits
herself to paper without having any idea of how or how quickly she will be able to pass on the note. An experienced person
would not manufacture and then hold on to incriminating evidence. The personal characteristics which she shows in this

monologue serve, then, to emphasize and develop certain traits which were in evidence in the previous act.

But what are we to make of the next scene (sc. 2), in which the feelings of Rosine and the Count for one another are brought out in discussion between Rosine and Figaro? The basic message of the scene is very simple: Figaro tells Rosine how 'his relative, Lindor' is in love with her, and she lets it be understood that she has similar feelings for him. But the tone and style of the conversation still maintain the ambiguous characterization of Rosine which we have seen so far. She must see that if Lindor has been lurking beneath her window, singing to her at her request, and is in love, then she is the person whom he is in love with. And yet she pretends that she is only very slowly realizing this as the conversation develops. Is she, then, a coquette savouring the pleasures of anticipation and the receiving of compliments, only to greet the news with feigned disbelief, before promptly acting upon it?

I think that a close reading of the conversation might suggest that she and Figaro are playing a *game,* which she initiates and he immediately takes up by answering her plain question, 'Avec qui parliez-vous donc là-bas si vivement?' with the exaggerated praise of someone whose identity he makes deliberately vague. It could be argued that, sensitive, lonely, intelligent, curious, but at the same time vulnerable and reticent, she naturally hides the fact of her intense interest in Lindor under the guise of a game, because in that way she is not obliged to risk appearing forward in front of Figaro, who is, after all, her social inferior (though she, like the Count, is not snobbish; l. 1754). The alternative strategy – to allow her to make her feelings explicit from the outset – would have made her look very forward, indeed, almost comically eager. If Rosine corresponds functionally to the Isabelle of the *parades,* it becomes all the more important for Beaumarchais to differentiate her in terms of character in the context of an intentionally more sophisticated comedy. (Whether he succeeds or not remains, of course, an open question.) It is also significant that the author underlines Rosine's emotion during this conversation with Figaro by stage directions: *étourdiment, vivement* (twice), *avec émotion, baissant les yeux, avec embarras.* This

could be taken to indicate that, even while playing a game
with Figaro and trying to keep her feelings from becoming too
apparent, she is still innocent inasmuch as she cannot fully
disguise them, and this would be the very antithesis of ruse
and coquettishness. Towards the end of the scene (after l. 493),
she has plainly admitted her interest in Lindor by passing
Figaro her letter. Are we to conclude, from her transparently
false claim that she is acting out of *pure amitié,* that she is still
unsure of the rightness of what she is doing or of Lindor's
trustworthiness, and that she simply wants to preserve her
retreat? This would, after all, be a perfectly reasonable strategy
for keeping her self-respect intact. Or is it just the manœuvre
of a flirt for preserving appearances if the situation backfires
on her? On the other hand, do we, as spectators, ever seriously
imagine that it will?

So far, then, we have seen Rosine both when she is showing
her feelings for Almaviva and when she is defending modern
times against Bartholo's retrograde views. In the former case,
her character is left open to more than one interpretation, but
in the latter Beaumarchais leaves no doubt; she is shown to
be both cunning (albeit in an unsophisticated way) and asser-
tive.

According to Descotes, for whom Rosine's main characteristic is spontaneity, *absence de calcul (19,* p. 94), Rosine's
character only appears puzzling if one judges her substantially
on the basis of her interactions with Bartholo. With her tutor
she is never really herself, but has instead to be always on her
guard, ready to defend herself. It is this pressure, according to
Descotes, that makes her appear both calculating and irritable.
This begs the question of what is meant by a dramatic character's 'real self' and looks to me like special pleading, but one
can see how the view might be justified. In act II, scene 4,
Rosine is unwilling at first to admit that she has seen Figaro,
but she is not artful and controlled enough to resist finally
acknowledging it. She tries to avoid answering Bartholo's
question by provoking an argument with him (ll. 545-46). But,
because she is not calculating *enough,* she is finally goaded by
his greater rudeness into losing her temper and giving away
the very piece of information which she knew she needed to

withhold. *Calcul* is not totally absent, but one concludes that she lacks the experience and self-mastery necessary to sustain it. She tries again to use Bartholo's irascibility in act II, scene 15, where, in order to make him forget the letter from Almaviva which she has just picked up, she sets out to quarrel with him over the opening of her mail. But Bartholo is typically too attentive and too astute to be fooled by this (typically) hastily improvised expedient. Nor was he fooled by her off-the-cuff excuses in II, 11 to account for Figaro's visit, her ink-stained finger and the missing paper. In that scene we see her blunder gauchely from one lie to the next, and in the end Bartholo abandons his inquiry in order to give her the advice: 'Pour qu'on vous crût, mon enfant, il faudrait ne pas rougir en déguisant coup sur coup la vérité; mais c'est ce que vous ne savez pas encore' (ll. 734-36). He then proceeds to guess the thoughts that must have gone through Rosine's mind with a fair degree of accuracy. The only successful one of Rosine's expedients is (thanks to Beaumarchais) the substitution of the letters in act II, scene 15, but in general her improvisations are failures. They indicate an inexperienced girl, and Bartholo's advice to her, whose accuracy she realizes only too well (see II, 16), confirms this analysis.

S. and J. Dauvin have discerned a limited kind of progress in Rosine's ability to handle awkward situations, especially those involving Bartholo (*18,* pp. 28-29). As proof of this they cite her exchange of letters (III, 4), her capacity for self-defence (II, 4), her ability to play a variety of parts (II, 15; III, 1 and 4), her use of double meanings (III, 12) and her exploitation of Bartholo's irascibility (II, 15). However, they do not see this progress in worldliness as undermining the picture of the *charmante enfant.* But one can't have it both ways; either she progresses and loses her ingenuousness, or she retains her ingenuousness, but doesn't progress. She comes out of the Dauvins' analysis as having made progress only because they call 'progress' a number of discrete events which are not cumulative at all. Also, in selecting their evidence, they leave out of account such obvious signs of unguarded spontaneity as Rosine's 'Ah!...' (III, 4, l. 1153) when she recognizes her lover through his disguise as Alonzo. Moreover, it is he, not she, who provides the explanation to Bartholo. This comes at a point when, according to the Dauvins, she was making progress in coping with her situation.

If we analyse Rosine's later appearances, it seems that, if anything, she becomes *less* cunning or worldly as the play goes on. In the 'stupefaction scene' (III, 11), she comes across as less inventive than the other characters, and all four of her contributions to the conversation repeat what another character has said before her, though admittedly the significance of this may be lessened by the fact that characterization was clearly less central to Beaumarchais's intentions in composing this scene than dramatic virtuosity was. A particularly telling scene is act IV, scene 3, where Bartholo produces the letter from Rosine which he had been given by the Count and invents Alonzo's betrayal of her. Here she is made to look excessively credulous. Why, knowing Bartholo's character and his dishonesty in other contexts, believe that he came by the letter in the way he claims he did, and why, when he has always been less kindly than Figaro and Lindor-Alonzo, suppose that his kindness and concern are genuine now? Disgusted by the apparent hypocrisy of Alonzo, Rosine acts with crass impulsiveness in promptly revealing Figaro's and Lindor-Alonzo's intentions to Bartholo and in agreeing to marry him.

If we look at the stage-directions which indicate her feelings as this scene unfolds – *étonnée, accablée, outrée, avec effroi, au désespoir* – we see that Beaumarchais is unmistakably stressing Rosine's *sensibilité,* possibly with a view to resolving the ambiguity which has surrounded her character up to this point. An emphasis on the quality of *sensibilité* (which was particularly in vogue in the literature of the time and was taken to indicate essential goodness) dominates all Rosine's appearances in the closing scenes of the play. A note of tender sadness breaks through the indignation of her challenge to Lindor (ll. 1757-65), shortly to be followed by a genuine faint. The scene closes with her refusal to contemplate revenge on Bartholo, and Beaumarchais carries this note of magnanimity through into the final scene, where Rosine, instead of gloating over Bartholo's undoing, only speaks once, and then laconically, in reply to a direct question from him (ll. 1857-58).

If we read the characterization of Rosine as one by which Beaumarchais tries to use every episode to bring out her admirable qualities and accept that her situation forces her to expedients which she would not otherwise adopt ('Mon excuse est dans mon malheur'), then the character has an inherent unity. If, on the other hand, one gives more weight to the evidence of forwardness and flirtatiousness, which is especially noticeable in the earlier parts of the play, then one will conclude that no such unity is achieved and that Beaumarchais is inconsistent in allowing Rosine to inherit some of the brazenness of her *parade* forbears and in trying to compensate for the impression this will make on the spectator by grafting on to the character the qualities of vulnerability and *sensibilité* and by adding bolt-on explanations for the morally dubious elements in the character (e.g. ll. 204-05, 219-20, 1029-32). The anonymous author of the *Observations* on the *Le Barbier de Séville, opéra-comique* wrote that 'le caractère de Rosine a deux nuances', seeing her at one point as a 'femme emportée par la contrainte et la passion', and at another as a 'petite personne timide' (*13,* p. 97). Broadly speaking, this is the same dichotomy as the one I have been outlining with regard to the Rosine of the comedy. And, to my mind, the most reasonable conclusion is that evidence of both trends in the character still persists, that Beaumarchais has failed in what appears to be an attempt to resolve the ambiguity, and that the characterization of Rosine is a patchwork.

Jacques Scherer points out (*30,* pp. 217-18) that a traitor-figure exists in all of Beaumarchais's plays, and in *Le Barbier* this role falls, not to Bartholo, who acts in constant pursuit of his own interests without actually betraying anyone, but to Bazile. Though the part is in fact a small one, Bazile is memorable. This is partly because he is the focus of the 'stupefaction scene', which struck contemporaries as particularly well-conceived, and partly because the character has come to acquire the almost mythical status of an incarnation of vileness, which culminated in the satanic interpretation of Edouard de Max in the period 1916-24 (see *19,* pp. 118-21). Others, however, notably Louis Jouvet, have seen him as the barest of the functional characters, present in only five of the play's forty-four scenes, and whose only significant contribution to the play lies in the lyrical but structurally inessential paean he sings to calumny (II, 8).

Before we ever meet him, Figaro describes him as 'un pauvre hère qui montre la musique à sa pupille, infatué de son art, friponneau, besogneux, à genoux devant un écu, et dont il sera facile de venir à bout' (I, 6). It is this character sketch – or assassination – that will be verified when we actually meet Bazile. The first we ever hear of him is in act I, scene 5, when Bartholo is impatiently awaiting his arrival because he is responsible for arranging the doctor's marriage for the following day. His position is that of organist at the Grand Couvent (as Alonzo later tells us; III, 2) and he is Rosine's music master. Ironically, it is he, then, who has put *La Précaution inutile* into her hands. His clothes and his post link him, like nearly all Beaumarchais's traitors, with the Church, and in the 'Préface' to *Le Mariage de Figaro* Beaumarchais was later to refer to him as 'l'abbé Bazile'.

When he makes his first appearance in act II, scene 8, it is not as a musician but as Bartholo's accomplice, though his speech is heavily imprinted with musical terminology. Although his speech on the efficacy of calumny is more notable as a piece of stylistic virtuosity on the author's part, it does work to characterize Bazile as a creature, subtle, cynical and dangerous, and as a member of a group of similar people operating on the fringes of society. This information assimilated, we are introduced to Bazile's major characteristic – and the one which will later prove crucial in bringing about the Count's and Rosine's marriage – his venality. This is presented in the comically unsuitable (but witty) terminology of musical harmony (ll. 655-58), and draws a contrastingly terse response, and payment, from Bartholo; 'cela s'appelle parler', says Bazile. The very brevity of this first appearance of Bazile conveys the impression of a busy, ubiquitous creature kept moving by timely injections of money.

Figaro's comments on Bazile which follow his exit (II, 9) slightly modify this boldly drawn picture without entirely reassuring the audience that Bazile's machinations will prove ineffectual. It flies in the face of experience to believe that fools are necessarily harmless, or that defamation will be ineffective simply because it originates from a disreputable source. By their very nature, rumours soon become detached from their sources, after all. On the other hand, an audience which has already come to know and like Figaro and has accepted the comic fantasy will, up to a point, be predisposed to take his reassurances into account, however groundless they would be in reality.

Bazile's next appearance, in the famous 'stupefaction scene' (III, 11), is as noteworthy as his previous one, although not principally for what it tells us about him. In fact, he is so nonplussed by the other characters' insistence, firstly that he should not speak, and then that he is ill, that Figaro's description of him as a *sot* seems to be borne out – although this is more a by-product of the author's masterly structuring of the scene than its main purpose. Predictably, the difficulty which Bazile's presence causes is resolved by the Count's playing on his venality; devoid of dignity, he is prepared to go along with a manœuvre which humiliates him, provided that he is adequately paid for it. Perhaps it is our uncertainty over whether Figaro is right in calling Bazile a fool, or whether Bazile is simply too venal to care if he appears one, that makes the character as sinister as the limits of a comedy allow.

His next appearance (IV, 1), in which characterization is not overshadowed by stylistic or structural features, suggests a greater degree of astuteness than we have seen in action previously. He is right in his deduction that the size of the bribe he received in act III, scene 11, indicates that the Count or one of his agents was at work, and the advice he gives Bartholo – to marry Rosine if he is really set on it, but in the full knowledge that she may be unfaithful if she is forced into marriage – makes sense even if it is grossly cynical. After a brief and gleeful reminder of his reliance on the power of calumny, he leaves in order to continue the preparations for Bartholo's marriage, unaware that on the basis of a plan laid in this scene he will effectively be thwarting it. This he duly does in scenes 7 and 8, where his incomprehension and venality operate yet again.

Cynical, shameless, servile, mercenary, Bazile is a strongly drawn character, a fantasized portrayal of Marin (according to Arnould (*13*, p. 34)) who had played a particularly ignoble role in the Goëzman affair and who achieved an unenviable immortality through Beaumarchais's *Mémoires,* where he is accused of having 'dénigré bassement' one honourable man and of having 'jeté du louche sur l'honnêteté' of another (*6*, p. 189).[9] Such activities are made to be typical of Bazile, and his references to the devil and hell, along with his use of repellent imagery (especially in II, 8) also contribute to the sinister and repugnant portrait of him. As with Figaro, so with Bazile, then, Beaumarchais makes considerable use of the technique of characterization which consists in adapting from a real-life model.

And yet, despite the evil with which the character is inevitably associated, and despite the fact that he is there to work against the outcome which every spectator hopes for, in general, Bazile is funny. He only ceases being funny if the role is interpreted on stage with the type of satanic emphasis used by de Max. The reason why we can find amusement in what is objectively such a sinister character is well formulated by M. Bouvier-Ajam, who writes, in 'Beaumarchais et la vérité historique':

> Le plus conventionnel [des personnages], en somme, serait encore Bazile, mais ce maître-fripon a de telles candeurs dans son amour immodéré de l'argent, qu'il contredit lui-même sa cynique doctrine et atténue par la pluralité de ses vices l'antipathie que le paroxysme d'un seul de ses vices engendrerait. (*21*, p. 90)

There is also another reason, I think, similarly connected with Bazile's worship of money. Bazile constantly sells himself in

---

[9] Beaumarchais attributed a number of Provençal words to Bazile in one of the manuscripts of the *Barbier* (Marin was a native of La Ciotat), but the censor, Arthaud, removed these, as he also removed Figaro's cry of *sacristain* at Bazile, leaving only the reference to *maringouins* (l. 147).

every way he can – as a spy, as a messenger, as a signatory – and in doing so he becomes a commercial object; he is reified. Reification is a basic satirical technique, and our normal reaction to satire is laughter.

The characterization of Bazile is achieved with broad brush strokes and has little of the complexity which distinguishes Figaro, Bartholo and Rosine. If he achieves prominence in the play it is either because all five of his appearances are in important scenes, of which two are particularly memorable, or because his part is liable to be enhanced by the interpretative technique of the actor who plays it. Louis Jouvet wrote of 'l'indigence dramatique de ce sinistre baladeur... personnage qui reste inexprimé', and Descotes sees him as basically a functional character (*19*, p. 116), and a close analysis seems to bear out their views.

It would be pointless to undertake a detailed examination of Beaumarchais's techniques of characterization for the remaining four characters: the two servants, the lawyer and the *alcade*. The lawyer is a conventional figure, used to avoid representing a priest on stage. Like many others before him, he has the professional tic of using legal terms in everyday conversation ('Sont-ce là les futurs conjoints?', l. 1809) and is so absorbed by legal procedures that he fails to understand reality ('Les demoiselles apparemment sont deux sœurs qui portent le même nom', ll. 1820-21). His comic obtuseness persists right to the end of the play. The servants are caricatures who exhibit a few obviously ludicrous traits and whose sole *raison d'être* is that they annoy Bartholo and hence amuse the audience. In this respect, they are similar to the *barbon*'s servants in a number of *parades,* and their dramatic affiliations are underlined by the inappropriateness of their names.

I mentioned earlier that it could be argued that Bartholo's autocratic treatment of his servants was possibly justified, though rather by the canons of a previous age. Jean Emelina takes the view that the comic servant's traditional shortcomings mark him out as one of an inherently inferior species. They validate the master's superiority and justify the scorn, insults and blows which the servant receives – even though both servant and master may be working towards the same goals (*20,* pp. 292-93). Bearing in mind that Bartholo is a *barbon* and a bourgeois, the antithesis and enemy of the comic hero, and does not fit into the general pattern of aristocratic hero and earthy servant which Emelina is describing, the tone of Bartholo's relationship with the servants is nonetheless similar in outline. The servants' stupidity balances (and frustrates) the master's intelligence, just as their childish naïveté balances his astuteness. He stands on his dignity – as a doctor and a householder, for example – whereas they have no dignity. The pattern which Emelina identifies as typical, in which master and servants each fulfil their assigned function in the ritual of oppression and submission, is exactly that of Bartholo and his servants.

To conclude on Beaumarchais's techniques of characterization, then, it could fairly be said that, while his protagonists exhibit a number of the traits which they inherit from their forbears in the Italian Theatre and the *parades,* Beaumarchais refines considerably on these models, and gives the main characters in the play a complexity and – save in the case of Rosine – a cohesion which can easily pass unrecognized. Except for Rosine, the main characters are constructed from a range of harmonious personality traits, which are clearly delineated over the first few scenes in which each appears. Without having the depth of Molière's protagonists, these characters do not come across as one-dimensional, but as complex creations moving against a background of fantasy. Rosine is the exception among the main characters in that the overlay of virtue and *sensibilité* which Beaumarchais has applied fails to hide the glad eye and the beckoning finger.

There is, however, some technical weakness in Beaumarchais's method of characterization in that it involves a high proportion of *telling* as opposed to *showing.* The typical application of this technique entails one character giving an off-the-cuff portrait of another, which is then borne out when this second character appears for the first time. The description of Bazile by Figaro (I, 6) and our first encounter with him in II, 8 are a case in point. Monologues or long speeches within conversations can also be used to convey essential background information or details about a character's state of mind, and hence to inform the audience of what it should think a character is 'really like'. Almaviva's soliloquy of I, 1 (which reads rather like a dialogue with an imaginary 'aimable de la cour') is the most striking example of a monologue which *tells* us everything. The autobiographical speech of Figaro (I, 2, ll. 142-61) runs a close second. Rosine is also made to confide her intimate feelings to the audience in monologues (e.g. II, 3) and, in II, 16, this goes so far as to look very much like an authorial attempt at resolving the audience's possible doubts about the basics of Rosine's character. Whereas with Figaro's speech, mentioned above, we actually 'feel' the exuberance of the personality in the account of his very active life, the depth of emotion and sensibility which Almaviva parades with an emphasis verging on mawkishness in I, 1 is not in evidence when the lovers are finally united in IV, 6, and when the Count *tells* Rosine that he *meurt d'amour*.

Beaumarchais constantly makes his characters tell one another – and hence the audience – what they feel. Sometimes he shows it as well; more usually not. On occasion, telling and showing are combined for emphasis, not always with very satisfying results. Thus, in IV, 6, for example, Rosine shows her emotional shock by a perfectly natural brief faint, but then goes on to spell out the related feelings explicitly: 'le plus affreux supplice n'est-il pas de haïr, quand on sent qu'*on est faite pour aimer?*' (ll. 1789-90); 'Voilà le fruit de *ma crédulité*' (ll. 1794-95 cf. ll. 1677-78) and: '*Mon cœur est si plein* que la vengeance ne peut y trouver de place' (ll. 1802-03; my italics). In fairness to Beaumarchais, it should be noted that this technique is not uncommon among eighteenth-century dramatists, even those with aspirations to psychological realism.

It has been argued (*16*, pp. 152-59) that psychological depth in the drawing of characters was not of primary or even of particular interest to Beaumarchais. For all their complexity and dramatic impact, they are not realistic. In the main, they are made to react to what each other says, to have battles of words, and generally relate to one another *à coups de dialogue*, without having sufficient psychological substance for us to imagine them to be capable of reacting convincingly 'from the heart'. And the explanation for this may well be that Beaumarchais aims not so much to delve into the recesses of the human mind as *to write memorably,* or, as Figaro puts it, to invent 'quelque chose de beau, de brillant, de scintillant, qui eût l'air d'une pensée'.

3

Dramatic Structures

W H E N Beaumarchais writes in the *Lettre modérée* that the plot of *Le Barbier* is that 'un vieillard amoureux prétend épouser demain sa pupille; un jeune amant plus adroit le prévient, et ce jour même en fait sa femme, à la barbe et dans la maison du tuteur', he is recalling the simple intrigues of a number of earlier works, chiefly but not exclusively theatrical, and some members of the audience would doubtless have been familiar with several of them. And yet, this deceptively simple summary gives no hint at all of the structural complexity of the play. Its gestation was relatively long and, as it passed through the different stages of its development, Beaumarchais gave it a structure whose constitutive elements interlock and balance one another to a rare degree.

A PLAY IN FOUR ACTS

The structure of *Le Barbier* is an amalgam of the regular and the almost unheard of. It was quite exceptional for a play to be divided into four acts. Beaumarchais's reasons for doing this are clear. Firstly, there is insufficient substance in the plot (contrast *L'Ecole des femmes*) to fill out five acts without either repetitions or the inclusion of extraneous material, as the five-act version proved. Secondly, Beaumarchais was more interested in writing something which audiences would applaud than in following structural models developed over a hundred years previously. The tradition of comedy, as evolved in the baroque and classical periods of the seventeenth century, had been to cast the play either in one act – a length

normally associated with farce – or in three acts, for plays in
the 'Italian' tradition, which did not generally aspire to do
more than to entertain – or in five acts, a length which denoted
a non-tragic but not wholly unserious play about contemporaries. The five-act structure was used by both Corneille and
Molière and served to imply, to an age which believed in a
hierarchy of literary genres, that comedy could reasonably lay
claim, in its treatment of modern subjects, to the dignity of
tragedy in its concern with the past.

Whereas the acts of a classical play were mostly of roughly
equal length (in Corneille's *La Suivante* (1633), they were of
exactly the same length), the first and last acts of *Le Barbier*
are shorter than acts II and III. The first act introduces the
main characters and sets the plot in motion; acts II and III
develop the imbroglio, and act IV brings the climax, with the
resolution of the lovers' misunderstanding and their immediate marriage. Beaumarchais's economy of one act is made
possible (indeed necessary) because his first act introduces the
main characters, lays down the parameters of the plot and
ushers in the difficulties which will need to be overcome. In
classical plays, the first *two* acts were habitually used in this
way. The imbroglios of acts II and III of *Le Barbier* correspond
broadly to the kind of action which occupied acts III and IV
of the five-act comedies, and the content of Beaumarchais's
fourth act, corresponds to what usually went into their fifth.

Distinctly post-classical too is the large number of scenes
per act. In the five-act classical comedies, the number of
scenes had averaged between twenty-five and forty, and the
eighteenth century saw a general increase on this. The usual
pattern had, broadly speaking, been for the number of scenes
per act to increase as the play moved towards its climax.
Even by eighteenth-century standards, Beaumarchais's scene-
changes are numerous. *Le Barbier* has forty-four scenes in its
four acts (6 + 16 + 14 + 8), and *Le Mariage* has ninety-two in
five (11 + 26 + 20 + 16 + 19). This compares, for example,
with the thirty-two of *L'Ecole des femmes* (1662) and the
sixty-nine of *Turcaret* (1709), both of which are in five acts.
The performance time of full-length plays was more or less
constant. Therefore, as each new scene means that a character

has entered or left the stage, an increase in the number of scenes implies a corresponding increase in the tempo, and that of *Le Barbier* is noticeably fast. Although Beaumarchais was thoroughly versed in classical French comedy, he is an innovator, not a revivalist. Despite their being staged at the Comédie Française, his plays have more structural affinities with the popular theatre of writers like Lesage (a prolific and successful author, most of whose output is no longer well-known) than with the better-known works performed at the Comédie Française.

THE ACTION

The total playing-time of *Le Barbier* is between 1½ and 1¾ hours, and much of the action which actually advances the plot obviously takes place out of sight of the audience. But let us begin by examining what kind of action is shown on stage and how it is structured.

The division of the play into acts is justified both on logistical grounds (trimming the candles) and dramatic ones, because each act clearly has a particular function within the total scheme, as outlined above. The same is not true, however, of the scene divisions, which occur with every entry and exit. Episodes in the action typically occupy not a single scene, but a series of scenes.

The whole of act I is a single unit. The main characters are introduced, their past and their relationships are outlined and their plans are laid. Thereafter, throughout the play, Beaumarchais uses a system of forward linking and recall to achieve dramatic unity both within and between the acts. Act II will serve as an example. In order to restart the theatrical illusion after the break between acts I and II, the first scene of the second act contains references to the fact that Marceline is ill (recalling Figaro's words of I, 4, ll. 290-91), to Rosine's *argus* and to the name Lindor. It is linked to scene 2 by Rosine's mention of Figaro, who promptly appears (as if by magic) and tells her that Lindor is a relative of his and is eager to meet her in person. Thereupon Rosine passes to Figaro the letter she was writing to Lindor in scene 1. Thematically these two scenes are linked to scenes 12 and 16, but their development is interrupted, initially by the series of scenes 3 to 8. These concern Bartholo's suspicions of his ward's contacts with Figaro, whose pharmaceutical inspirations have incapacited the household, and with the tutor's collusion with Bazile to arrange his marriage for the following day. Scenes 9 and 10 go together, and in them Rosine learns of Bartholo's marriage-plan from Figaro, who witnessed scenes 3 to 8 from his hidding-place. Scene 11 stands alone, and shows Bartholo's inquisitorial bullying of Rosine on the basis of his well-founded suspicions. Taking up again the theme prepared in scenes 1 and 2, scenes 12 to 16 form a single episode in which Lindor, disguised as a drunken soldier, enters and manages to exchange letters with Rosine. Bartholo goes to considerable trouble to read Lindor's, but is tricked into reading an innocuous substitute, and the act ends with Rosine reading Lindor's real letter.

The scheme of the scenes within act II could therefore be expressed in the following way, which demonstrates its link with act I, the sequences within it and the method by which it achieves overall structural cohesion.

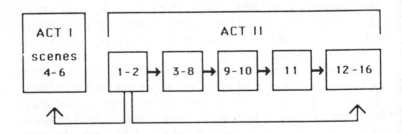

An analysis of act III would show how the first scene recalls Rosine's calmness after the letter episode of II, 15 (ll. 1007, seq.) and her subsequent reading of Lindor's letter, and that the action of scenes 3 to 10, suspended by the stupefaction scene, resumes in scenes 12 to 14. Again, the diagrammatic representation of the structure of the act brings out its dramatic unity.

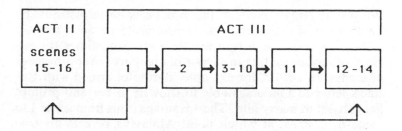

Like act I, act IV is a single unit devoted to the unfolding of a single dramatic episode. Just as the exposition was rapid and economical, so is the *dénouement*. In scene 1 Bartholo and Bazile agree to bring forward the doctor's marriage, aware that Almaviva and Figaro are working to forestall it. They hit upon the expedient of divulging to Rosine Bartholo's possession of her letter to Lindor, and Bazile leaves to fetch the notary. In scenes 2 and 3 Bartholo comes upon Rosine waiting for Lindor to climb in through the casement (with its exceptionally convenient *external* key-hole), and, producing the letter, he suggests that Lindor was simply procuring her for Almaviva, whereupon, in order to redeem her self-respect, she agrees to marry the doctor.

The action accelerates even more from this point on, and the climax is reached in the series of scenes 4 to 8. Rosine confronts Almaviva and Figaro, and the truth is explained, with the Count revealing his real identity (sc. 6). A perpetually puzzled Bazile is bribed (again) into witnessing the signing of the marriage-contract before the equally puzzled notary (sc. 7). Bartholo returns to a *fait accompli* (sc. 8) and has to be content with escaping an investigation of his maladministration of Rosine's fortune. With the recalls of previous elements in the play (Bazile's venality, Bartholo's dishonesty, etc.), the progress of the plot of act IV is strictly linear, while that of the action depends on the absence of Bazile and Bartholo during the middle scenes of the act.

Looking at the internal structure of the sequences of scenes, we find that dramatic tension is maintained by peripeteia (reversals) which tilt the balance of advantage alternately between Bartholo-and-Bazile and the Almaviva-Figaro-Rosine trio.

Within the fantasy context, this process is made plausible by the balance of intelligence and perspicacity between the two sides, with Bazile as a transferable asset. Sometimes the balance of advantage tilts in favour of one party over a number of scenes. In act IV, for example, Bartholo, armed with Rosine's letter to Lindor, is able to show it to her and prompt her consent to marry him. The advantage is his from scene 1 to scene 6, l. 1775, at which point Almaviva reveals his true identity, and Rosine realizes that Bartholo has tricked her. From then on the advantage is predominantly with the Count.

Within that overall scheme, Beaumarchais introduces what Scherer has called *péripéties-éclair* (see *30,* ch. 5), momentary reversals of the balance of advantage and disadvantage which succeed and cancel one another rapidly. One example of this follows immediately on the episode I have just outlined, with the arrival of Bazile in scene 7. We expect that, being in league with Bartholo, he will raise the alarm and prevent the marriage. *But* he is typically perplexed and, above all, venal, *therefore* his untrustworthiness can be turned to advantage by paying him to witness the signing of the contract. S. and J. Dauvin note five of these *retournements de situation* in II, 14 alone (see *18,* pp. 48-49).

As well as using the technique of reversal to create and maintain dramatic tension, Beaumarchais also uses the juxtaposition of scenes crucial to the development of the plot and scenes largely devoted to eliciting laughter. The most obvious example occurs in act II, scenes 5, 6 and 7, in which Bartholo's servants, puerile, incapacitated and argumentative, exasperate their master. These three scenes provide comic relief after the four tense scenes involving the interview between Rosine and Figaro, in which the crucial letter to Lindor changes hands (scenes 1 and 2), Rosine gives vent to her anxieties (scene 3), and Bartholo interrogates her over the dropped song (scene 4). They directly precede the cynicism of the 'calumny scene' (scene 8), in which Bartholo and Bazile evolve a dishonourable scheme, with Figaro hiding in the closet. While we laugh at the interlude with the obtuse servants, we carry at the back of our minds the tension created by the first four scenes of the act, which we half-suspect will be heightened in the eighth, as indeed it is. Moreover, the tense scenes themselves vary in tone from worrying and undercover planning to ruthless interrogation and overt quarrelling.

THE SETTING

Jacques Scherer appositely encapsulated Beaumarchais's conception of the theatre when he wrote that: 'La pièce de théâtre est pour lui une composition. Plus les éléments qu'elle compose sont variés, efficaces et nombreux, plus grande est la tension provoquée "dans l'âme du spectateur" et plus grand l'intérêt' (*30*, p. 143). By *intérêt*, we should understand the spectator's emotional and intellectual involvement in what he sees happening on stage. We have already seen how character portrayal draws the spectator emotionally into the events depicted. In the opening scenes, for example, Figaro's exuberance has the effect of engaging our complicity in his enterprise. With Bartholo, the same mechanism operates in reverse.

But in *Le Barbier* there is a large measure of intellectual and aesthetic involvement too, and the author uses a range of devices to bring this about. The visual aspect of the play, comprising costume and setting, is the first and perhaps one of the clearest examples. Beaumarchais stipulated the characters' costumes in detail, both for purposes of characterization and to give the play an unmistakably Spanish look, later to be reinforced in conversations involving Spanish place-names, professions and forms of address.

It is, of course, a fake, and an admitted fake. Whether audiences knew it or not, Figaro's and Almaviva's costumes come from two different periods. The Count's had been abolished in Spain by a decree of 1766, whereas Figaro is dressed in the latest fashion. The habit of serenading ladies to the accompaniment of a guitar was indeed more typically Spanish than Parisian, but the setting on two levels – the balcony overhanging the street – was the familiar disposition of actors and audiences for the French *parades*. Bartholo may be nominally a Spanish doctor, but the figures of doctor, ageing tutor and thwarted old lover lay clearly within French or naturalised

French theatrical traditions, and all the innovations which Bartholo dislikes were either supra-national or specifically *French*.

The Franco-Spanish hybrid is a never-never land, which the author invites us to see as such. And, in addition to the costumes and setting, he also uses the carefully manipulated improbability of the plot, as well as brief interruptions of the theatrical illusion with remarks such as: 'Nous ne sommes pas ici en France, où l'on donne toujours raison aux femmes' (ll. 953-54), and: 'toutes ces histoires de maîtres supposés sont de vieilles finesses, des moyens de comédie' (ll. 1122-23). Clearly, to Beaumarchais a play was not only *une composition,* but also *un jeu.*

TIME

The duration of the action is rather less than twenty-four hours. It opens in the very early morning, while the streets are still quiet and the windows shuttered, and continues until sometime between midnight and 4 a.m. on the following day. Allusions to the approach of the fatal moment of Rosine's marriage to Bartholo are frequent – especially the word *demain,* and this gives a sense of urgency to the Count's plan to free Rosine from her tutor and marry her himself. Act IV particularly, which opens in darkness, contains a number of time-references, such as *minuit, quatre heures* and *cette nuit même.*

Within this scheme of signposts the spectator's more subliminal awareness of the passage of time comes from the duration of the exchanges and the impression one gets of how long it would actually take to accomplish things which are planned in one scene and subsequently referred to as done. The passage of time is also implied, for example, by Bartholo's falling asleep in act III, scene 4. If, as he says, his tiredness is the result of his medical duties, we automatically assume that these have taken up a large portion of the day and that this is to be located in the intervals between acts I and II, and II and III; this time-scale is in fact confirmed by Bazile's *bonsoir* of act III, scene 11.

The action of act I is continuous and seemingly runs from around daybreak to just after. There are no time-lapses between the scenes, and no one leaves in order to set other action in motion before the end of the act. Therefore the action implies no longer duration than the time it takes to act. The largest part of the day – some ten hours from early morning to early evening – therefore stretches through act II up to act III, scene 1.

A lapse of time is clearly implied between acts I and II. Rosine's opening words, 'Marceline est malade', recall Figaro's plan outlined in act I, scene 4 (ll. 287-91), and we find Bartholo angry in act II, scene 4 because Figaro had bled her from the foot (l. 524). If the entry of Figaro in scene 2 and of Bartholo in scene 4 follow without a pause from the preceding scenes, then clearly the time-lapse implied between acts I and II is considerable. It is long enough for Figaro to go to his shop, fetch his medical kit, perform four medical interventions in three different parts of the house, return his kit to his shop, come back and appear in Rosine's room. Bartholo has meanwhile, presumably, been visiting patients on foot and has had the time also to come home and discover the havoc Figaro has caused. The remaining scenes of the act (5-16) follow on with no implied break.

The implied time-lapse between acts II and III is seemingly rather longer than that of the previous break between acts. The Count has had time to leave Bartholo's house, return to his lodging in the Grande Place, effect a removal, change disguises and return, while Rosine has had time to find a pretext and pick a further quarrel with Bartholo, who will himself have been away from the house for part of the time. The unpaused *enchaînement* of each of the scenes of act III is clear from the text, and the next lapse of time is suggested by the onset of darkness between acts III and IV.

What is notable about the temporal structure of acts II and III and the three intervals is that the visible action moves so swiftly that when a character leaves to perform a specific task he cannot return in the same act without obvious implausibility. Beaumarchais therefore has to delay his return until the longer time-lapse between two acts has passed. For example, Bazile has told Bartholo that the Count is in Seville and is lodging in the Grande Place (II, 8), and before he leaves he tells Bartholo that he will spend the whole day working on the arrangements for the doctor's marriage. It is in the next act (scene 11) that he is able to announce that the Count has left his lodging, a fact which only the interval would have allowed him to discover, given the speed of the visible action of act II, scenes 9 to 16 and act III, scenes 1 to 10. The disabling of Bartholo's servants and mule, placed between act I, scene 4 (Figaro's idea) and act II, scene 4 (Bartholo's complaints) is a similar case. Beaumarchais's use of the intervals between acts is subtle. He allows himself to construct rapid and uninterrupted sequences of scenes, in which the dialogue and the action must of necessity quite often do almost nothing to advance the plot (hence the frequency of peripeteia), and the action which is instrumental to the advancement of the plot is moved into the nineteen or so 'unaccounted' hours which the play encompasses.

Some five or six hours appear to separate acts III and IV, and the latter opens with the stage in darkness and a storm raging outside. In this forbidding atmosphere a conspiratorial conversation takes place between Bartholo and Bazile, by the light of a (waterproof?) paper lantern. It is not until the sympathetic trio of Figaro, the Count and Rosine, is in the house that all the candles are lit and the gloom dispelled (scene 6), a single (sinister) candle having, one presumes, been all the illumination for scene 3.

Whereas the time required for the activity of acts I, II and III could spill over into the intervals, the plot has to be resolved in act IV without any recourse to 'implied' time. Two remarks delimit the real time available: Rosine's 'il est minuit sonné' (l. 1650), and Figaro's retort to the *alcalde,* after the contract has been signed, that it is 'aussi près du matin que du soir' (ll. 1844-45). This second remark seems to situate the time somewhere around 2 a.m. [10]

---

[10] According to Bonneville (*2,* p. 142, n. 3), Figaro means that it is now 4 a.m. This cannot be correct, since the notary, who was due at 4 a.m., has been fetched early, and one cannot reasonably assume that the errands of Bazile and Bartholo would take almost four hours to accomplish.

We learn in scene 1 that Bazile has planned to bring the notary (who works singularly unsocial hours) to Bartholo's house for 4 a.m., which was the earliest time he could manage because he had been retained by Figaro to perform another marriage immediately before Bartholo's. Shortly after midnight, the conversation between Bartholo and Rosine takes place during which he produces her letter to Lindor. Bartholo departs immediately afterwards in search of a law-enforcement officer, and only moments separate his exit from the entry of the Count and Figaro. They have presumably left the notary at Figaro's house (scene 3, l. 1736), and it is from there that Bazile brings him to Bartholo's in scene 7. Since Figaro's house is nearby, the time needed for fetching the notary appears feasibly equivalent to the time taken by events on stage. Bartholo's absence in search of the officers lasts throughout the lovers' quarrel and explanations, the return of Bazile with the notary and the rapid signing of the contract. Again we have the impression that what is happening offstage would take the same time as the action we see, and none of the offstage action implies a precise duration. Bazile's errand to Figaro's house, which also implies a conversation between himself and the notary, and Bartholo's fetching of the officers are temporally unquantifiable. Though Beaumarchais does not attempt to avoid implausibility in several other aspects of the play (the story, the role of Chance, disguises, etc.), his handling of time is notably realistic.

THEATRICAL SPACE

From the nascent classical period up to the advent of melodrama, 'high culture' French plays were generally fixed in a single location, whether it was the *palais à volonté* of tragedy or the private house of comedy. The idea behind this single setting is *vraisemblance*. Given that the period of time covered by the events of a play was ideally to be no more than twenty-four hours, it could not reasonably occupy locations which were too numerous or too dispersed. Generally, this single focus of the action presented no real constraint. If some element of the action could not take place within the single location, the most frequent solution was to report it, and simply refer to the other location. In other instances, however, this would prove dramatically unsatisfactory – as when one character needs to be near enough to the action on stage to spy on another. One solution to this problem is to compartmentalize the stage. The 'wall' of the 'compartment' may be real, like the tablecloth sometimes used in performances to conceal Orgon in *Tartuffe* (IV, 5), or the chair where, first Chérubin and then the Count seek to hide in *Le Mariage de Figaro*. Alternatively, it may simply consist in the fact that one character on stage is not looking towards another character who is doing something surreptitiously. Both of these devices have the effect of extending the space available for the action of the play. The first type of space – when the extra location is simply referred to – can conveniently be called implied space, and the second type – when the stage is in some way divided or partitioned –created or invented space. *Le Barbier* provides ample illustration of both types.

Even the most cursory reading of the text reveals the author's frequent use of implied space, in which a great deal of the action which furthers the plot is carried on. It extends into the town, with the Count's lodging in the Grande Place, Bazile's sacristy and the notary's office, and comes nearer with Figaro's shop, which is only a stone's throw from Bartholo's house. Sometimes the place is only the imagined other end of a journey which one of the characters must make (the sacristy, for example), while at other times it is the focus for action which we are left to imagine. We imagine Bazile skulking near the Count's lodging and the Count's hasty departure from it between acts III and IV. Figaro's shop is certainly visited by him and the Count in the intervals between acts. These are places where the intrigue is furthered and where characters wait, hide, or are sometimes observed. In order for the action to remain intelligible, only the *planning* of it needs to be done in the sight of the audience.

Other areas of implied space lie within Bartholo's house and are most often the locus of activity which one character must either temporarily or permanently conceal from another.

Figaro visits the stables in order to disable Bartholo's mule (the normal mode of transport for all but the richest eighteenth-century doctors) and the servants' quarters to administer drugs to La Jeunesse and L'Eveillé. The stables are seemingly visited also by Bartholo. Figaro visits Marceline's room and effectively confines her to it. A prison for Marceline, it is proposed by Bartholo as a refuge for Rosine against the 'invasion' of the rest of the house by the Count in act IV – confirming our impression of Bartholo's locked, bolted, barred (but comically penetrable) house as a fortress with a keep.

Bartholo's own rooms (*chambre* and *cabinet*) are implied in act III, scenes 5 to 8, and he is reluctant to let anyone into them. They are locked, and Figaro is allowed into the *cabinet*, Bartholo's most private 'den', only with the impolite instruction 'mais ne touchez à rien' (sc. 7). Bartholo's reluctance underlines not only his generally suspicious turn of mind, but also (especially since his bureau is also mentioned) reminds us that he keeps compromising papers there, particularly those relating to his management of Rosine's property. Between Bartholo's room and Rosine's sitting-room is a stairway. Out of sight of the other characters, Figaro is able to 'pinch' *(accrocher)* a key there and divert attention by smashing the porcelain shaving-kit, on the pretext that he had caught *(accroché)* his sleeve on a key (left in a lock in *Bartholo*'s house?). Bartholo's rooms and the adjacent stairway are a focus of intense action, just out of sight. The crucial theft has to be perpetrated, and quickly, because Figaro must not be absent too long, and the darkness of the stairway must be noted and immediately used as an excuse for the fake accident which will divert Bartholo's attention from the key-ring from which the shiniest key is now missing.

The closet, the *cabinet du clavecin*, is also implied space, along with the service stairway or back stairs to which it gives access. The *cabinet* is of particular significance in that its interior is invisible from Rosine's sitting-room, which allows it to be used as a hiding-place, but it is near enough to be within earshot of the sitting-room and can therefore be used for eavesdropping. Figaro enters the closet in act II, scene 2 to avoid being intercepted by Bartholo, stays concealed during

Bartholo's encounters with Rosine, L'Eveillé and La Jeunesse, and overhears the discussion of the tutor's marriage plans with Bazile (II, 8), before re-emerging in scenes 9-10 and leaving by the back stairs at the end of scene 10. The closet in this instance functions in the same way as the split setting of casement and street did in act I, where Figaro and Almaviva could hide and overhear the exchanges between Bartholo and Rosine. Although the invisible rooms and stairways of the house clearly come within my definition of implied space, they are different from, say, Figaro's house, since they give immediate access to the focal location of the action and are within earshot. As we have seen, both these conditions are exploited in act II, scene 8, but that particular scene is important too in that it illustrates the exploitation of created or invented space.

The stage-directions tell us that Figaro is 'caché dans le cabinet [et] paraît de temps en temps et les [Bartholo et Bazile] écoute'. Whenever he appears, unseen by the villains, the stage becomes in effect divided between two actions carried on simultaneously. New space is created for the action 'Figaro eavesdropping and learning vital information', while the action 'Bartholo and Bazile plotting to denigrate the Count and hasten the doctor's marriage to Rosine' unfolds in the foreground. Another form of created space is used in act II, scene 15, where Bartholo uses the chair to divide the stage space in order to read the letter which Rosine has concealed without her seeing him. In this instance the situation is complicated by the fact that the substitute letter and bogus faint make recourse to created space seem necessary but prove fruitless (cf. also III, 12). Failing the imposition of an obstacle to vision, the characters may need to have recourse to sleight of hand, as the Count does in order to pass Rosine his letter during the moments when Bartholo is taking his billeting exemption from the desk in act II, scene 14.

The tension which brings the need to create and exploit new space is well illustrated in act III, scene 5. The scene begins with a divided space; Bartholo is singing and dancing, and Figaro is parodying him behind his back. But, once this moment is over (when Bartholo sees and greets Figaro), our attention focuses on the lovers' need to talk and their vain attempts to do so while Bartholo and Figaro argue about the drugging of the servants, the outstanding rent and the imaginary sweets for Figaro's daughter. But, as Beaumarchais indicates in the stage direction (ll. 1320-23), the fact that Bartholo is able to argue with Figaro while at the same time watching the Count prevents the formation of the barrier which would allow two sets of action to take place simultaneously in the one setting.

At times when the kinds of spatial division of the scene I have been describing cannot be contrived, the need for such division can be satisfied by recourse to *aparté*. When it is impossible to conceal the fact that a verbal exchange is occurring, those involved are forced to lower its volume so that a third party (but not the audience) cannot hear it. The speakers have to accept the risk that the *fact* of conversation may be perceived, but seek still to preserve the secrecy of its content (e.g. ll. 1544-45) – the stupefaction scene (III, 11) also contains several examples of this – and in the same scene we see the removal of an obstacle immediately followed by the interception of a low-volume conversation (stage-direction, ll. 1554-55). Another example, unusual in that it is Rosine that is being 'curtained off' from a low-key exchange between Bartholo and Almaviva, occurs in act III, scene 4 (ll. 1204-06). When circumstances prevent even *aparté,* the division becomes purely intellectual or notional and relies on double meaning, as in the use of the words *lettre* (ll. 830-32) and *accrocher* (ll. 1452-56). [11]

Disguise too can be seen as another method for creating space; the concealing 'wall' becomes a transportable personal

---

[11] Division of the scenic space is not, of course, the *only* function of the aside. Beaumarchais also uses it for underlining an action which is crucial but not easily visible from the auditorium – e.g. Rosine hiding her cousin's letter for Bartholo to 'find' – or for indicating that out-loud speech is the cover for or antithesis of what a character is thinking. In this second function, it is arguably less than necessary, but it is nonetheless a traditional device for amusing audiences, and is still used nowadays.

envelope. It gives all the advantages of the hiding-place; it also allows movement, communication and participation. But it carries increased risks of recognition, self-betrayal and being trapped – as the Count is acutely aware.

4

Language and Music

J u s t as rapid movement marks the actions of the characters and hence the structure of the scene sequences, so it also marks the dialogue. This does not 'simply happen'. It results from the author's conscious and sustained effort to achieve *concision*. The evidence of this effort is readily available in Arnould's *Genèse (13)*, where four stages in the elaboration of the text are published together. Because Beaumarchais's preoccupation with concision substantially rules out many of those elements which would serve to individualize a character's manner of speech (contrast Molière), leaving only the minimum number of words needed to convey a meaning, all the characters speak in broadly the same way, and such differentiation as there is at a linguistic level largely results from the use of personal images. Bazile's use of musical and diabolical metaphor are illustrations of this, as is the terminology of Rosine's references to the contrast between the freedom she desires (III, 4, the song) and the situation she lives in (ll. 169-70, 205, 545-46).

One of the most frequent of Beaumarchais's economies consists simply in omitting superfluous words. This is the case, for instance, in the exchange between Figaro and the Count in act I, scene 4, ll. 223-30 ('Te voilà instruit [...] une jeune personne d'une beauté! ...'). It is clear that 'si tu jases...' could *only* be followed by a threat of some kind. Not only is it therefore unnecessary to formulate it, but, were it in fact formulated, it would overload and *sour* a dialogue devoted to showing a friendly relationship. The 'Moi, jaser!' is the most economical formulation of the idea 'Jaser serait contre mon intérêt personnel, je ne le ferais donc pas', and the economy of Beaumarchais's expression here allows him space to deve-

lop the (rather unexciting) idea that ritualized assurances of
devotion are debased social currency – a general observation
which, while it contributes nothing vital to the main drift of
the dialogue, at least does not overload the reply, as it would
do if the rest of the exchange were less concise. The 'et...' of
Figaro's second speech (l. 228) was followed in an earlier
version by the suppressed 'personne ne vous trompera' – a sen-
tentious banality which, from an aesthetic point of view, is best
omitted. Similarly, whatever might follow 'd'une beauté!...'
could only be something of the force of 'que je ne saurais
décrire' and is therefore unnecessary.

Ellipsis, when it is reduplicated, is not only very economical with words, but also amusing. Beaumarchais uses it in act
IV, scene 1 (ll. 1636-38):

> BARTHOLO   Ce drôle est du complot: que diable!...
> BAZILE   Est-ce que vous penseriez...?
> BARTHOLO   Ma foi, ces gens-là sont si alertes!

There are in fact three truncated sentences here, which,
if fully formulated, would merely make the play more prolix
without making the ideas clearer.

Another of Beaumarchais's methods for making the dialogue rapid and succinct is to have one character use a single
reply to answer an interlocutor's question and himself pose
another question, or make a statement which will elicit another
question (see, for example, IV, 1, ll. 1629-36). Verbal economy
is also achieved by the use of questions phrased so as to allow
the person answering implicitly to confirm or deny a premise
by giving further information which makes the (unexpressed)
direct answer to the question obvious (e.g. II, 4, ll. 529-31).
While the frequency of any one 'technique of economy' may
be limited enough to escape immediate notice, cumulatively
they contribute a great deal to shortening the play and increas-
ing the density of the dialogue.

Whereas he aims for economy when this can be achieved
without detriment to the sense, Beaumarchais allows himself
increased spread where a further comic effect or richer characterization can result from it. This happens, for instance, when

one character 'hijacks' a sentence begun by another, for example:

BAZILE	Et puis, comme dit le proverbe, ce qui est bon à prendre...
BARTHOLO	J'entends, est bon...
BAZILE	...à garder.
BARTHOLO, *surpris*	Ah! ah!
BAZILE	Oui, j'ai arrangé comme cela plusieurs petits proverbes avec des variations. Mais allons au fait... (ll. 1602-07)

Here, the interruption is reinterrupted immediately, and the momentary diversion in the conversation is used both as a further illustration of Bazile's character (gleeful cynicism) and of his literary pastimes, as well as an elegant and amusing piece of wordplay (cf. also I, 2, ll. 86-92).

Beaumarchais's pleasure in manipulating words and sounds is consistently obvious. Figaro's description of Bartholo (ll. 248-50) relies more on an arrangement of sounds to convey a meaning than it does on the definitions of the words used, and Beaumarchais's effort to maximize the effect while minimizing the length is evidenced by a comparison with the earlier stages which the description passed through (see *13*, p. 169). The portrait was at some stages in its development overcharged with plainly ludicrous elements and forced jokes, none of which is particularly amusing, and their cumulative effect is tedious. It is a measure of Beaumarchais's mastery of dramatic language that he was able in the end to select from the mass of verbiage the more inspired opening portion, with its mixture of assonance, nonsense and evocative power. Economy is again the key to the success of the language in that it says enough to achieve the desired effect, and no more.

Gabriel Conesa, in his *commentaires* appended to the Livre de Poche edition of the text (*3*, p. 141), singles out as an illustration of 'le travail exigeant d'un écrivain conscient de son art' the process which the original form of the following remark by Figaro went through before achieving its final interplay of rhythm and assonance:

1) Je voudrais finir par quelque chose de brillant, de claquant...
2) ...de beau, de brillant, de claquant, de scintillant...
3) ...de beau,   de brillant,   de scintillant...

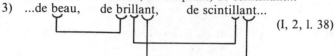

(I, 2, l. 38)

Given the speed of the dialogue, these stylistic refinements will often elude the intellectual analysis of the spectator (though hopefully not of the reader) and instead create the overall impression of an aesthetically pleasing, rhythmical and harmonious flow of words. This is a key factor in making the language specifically *dramatic*.

Binary oppositions in which each antithetical element is cast in a similar form also occur in *Le Barbier*. They are immediately perceptible and – often because they have a proverbial ring to them – memorable. Figaro's life-story (I, 2), for example, contains the sentences: 'l'amour des lettres est incompatible avec l'esprit des affaires' (ll. 104-05) and: 'l'utile revenu du rasoir est préférable aux vains honneurs de la plume' (ll. 151-52). Similarly, Bartholo's reply to Bazile in act IV, scene 1: 'Il vaut mieux qu'elle pleure de m'avoir, que moi je meure de ne l'avoir pas' (ll. 1617-18) contains groups of oppositions reinforced by assonance.

The strong rhythmic pattern of the accumulation of groups of words having the same syntactical structure can be revealed by a count of the pronounced syllables of a given speech. Take, for example, Figaro's closing words to the Count in act I, scene 6 (ll. 400-04):

> Moi, j'entre ici (4) (où), par la force de mon art (6), (je vais), d'un seul coup de baguette (6), endormir la vigilance (7), éveiller l'amour (5), égarer la jalousie (7), fourvoyer l'intrigue (5), et renverser tous les obstacles (8). Vous, Monseigneur (4), (chez moi) l'habit de soldat (5), le billet de logement (6), et de l'or dans vos poches (6).

Discounting the unemphasized introductory phrases which are placed in parentheses, the syllable pattern is revealed as 4,6,6,7,5,7,5,8,4,5,6,6. The rhythmic pattern is strong and reminiscent of a song, an incantation or a spell, or possibly the patter of a mountebank. Such symmetrical effects are normally confined in *Le Barbier* to the speeches of a single character and are only exceptionally carried into a series of replies coming from different speakers. Beaumarchais and his contemporaries generally avoided the kind of stylized symmetry of dialogue such as we find Molière using in M. Purgon's 'cursing' of Argan, for instance (*Le Malade imaginaire,* III, 5). Conesa makes this point (*16,* p. 35) and refers to the stylized quarrel between Trissotin and Vadius in *Les Femmes savantes,* III, 3, where the symmetry is emphasized particularly by the versification. While avoiding the visible artificiality of sustained, symmetrical dialogue, Beaumarchais does not avoid short, symmetrical exchanges such as sometimes occur in everyday conversation, especially where – humorously or otherwise – one interlocutor is being rude to the other. In act II, scene 13 (ll. 806-07) the Count develops what Bartholo has said about medicine and uses a parallel structure in order to do so: 'Un art dont le soleil s'honore d'éclairer les succès – Et dont la terre s'empresse de couvrir les bévues.'

Conesa points out that *tirades,* which are relatively rare in Beaumarchais's works, are virtuoso pieces. They are not usually linked directly to the development of the plot but are introduced, unfold and conclude within the structure of a dialogue which resumes its course once the *tirade* is over. The hymn to calumny (II, 8) is the most obvious case in *Le Barbier.* Introduced by the idea 'susciter une méchante affaire... et pendant la fermentation, calomnier', it is integrated into the dialogue by the idea '[il faut éviter de] se compromettre' and by Bartholo's questioning of its relevance to his own situation. (It is arguably less irrelevant than he thinks; see *19,* p. 114.) Similarly, Figaro's autobiography (I, 2, ll. 142-61) is framed by an implied question ('Mais tu ne me dis pas...') and a direct one ('Qui t'a donné une philosophie aussi gaie?'), but it is constructed as an autonomous piece out of accumulations and binary oppositions. (The framing technique is one which Beaumarchais typically uses for integrating witticisms and 'philosophical' remarks.) Neither of these *tirades* is without a psychological function, clearly, but their main impact is an aesthetic one and turns on the pleasure we derive from displays of verbal *panache*.

Succinctness, balance and rhythm are notable characteristics of the language of the play, but equally obvious are the aphorisms – often socio-political in content – with which the dialogues are punctuated. The substance of Beaumarchais's socio-political comments in *Le Barbier* goes no further than the philosophical commonplaces of his time: 'un grand nous fait assez de bien quand il ne nous fait pas de mal' (ll. 107-08), 'Aux vertus qu'on exige dans un domestique, Votre Excellence connaît-elle beaucoup de maîtres qui fussent dignes d'être valets?' (ll. 114-16), 'Les vrais magistrats sont les soutiens de ceux qu'on opprime' (ll. 1877-78). Other contemporaries were often more audacious, and Clément Borgal's classification of Beaumarchais's *sentences* as *miettes philosophiques* is not inappropriate (*15,* ch. 4).

Like many other writers, Beaumarchais was in the habit of recording witticisms and pithy turns of phrase and of subsequently incorporating them into his creative writings. Sometimes, especially in the cases of Figaro and Bazile, they can be made to contribute to characterization, and this gives them an appearance of naturalness, even when they are not strictly germane to the conversation in progress. Figaro's well-known 'goddam' speech, which now figures in *Le Mariage* (III, 5), was originally incorporated into *Le Barbier,* for example. Similarly, Figaro's turning his back on Bartholo with the quip about always giving in in disputes with fools (ll. 1375-78) figures in the author's notebook in the form:

> – Quand je dispute avec un obstiné, je ne lui cède jamais.
> – Et moi, je lui cède toujours. Adieu.   (*7,* p. 105)

Though the authorial contrivance is not usually apparent, occasionally one becomes aware of it. 'Quand on cède à la peur du mal, on ressent déjà le mal de la peur' (II, 2, ll. 478-79), seems to be one such case. Slightly forced and pedantic, it reveals the author behind the dramatic character. But there is no reason to suppose that Beaumarchais would have thought this a fault.

MUSIC

As I indicated earlier, one of the stages in the evolution of the play was that of an *opéra-comique*. Traces of this stage in its development are still apparent in its final form. The roles of all the main characters except the real music teacher, Bazile, contain some singing. To modern ears, the songs and sung snatches probably have considerable aesthetic appeal – especially Almaviva's 'Vous l'ordonnez...' of act I, scene 6 – they certainly do not seem misplaced, in any case. And yet, Beaumarchais had the greatest difficulty in persuading the Comédie Française to accept them. The objection was raised that singing lowered the dignity of the 'top' theatre, and, after the failure of the five-act version, Rosine's ariette 'Quand, dans la plaine...' (III, 4) was omitted from the performance when the play was recast in four acts – much to Beaumarchais's regret (see *10*, p. 442, n. 74).

To provide aesthetic pleasure through the purely musical appeal of the songs was not, however, Beaumarchais's only reason for including them. Frequently they are used to tell the audience something about the character who sings them. But this information does not lie on the verbal surface. Where Beaumarchais has taken tunes from other works and set new words to them, the words associated with the tune in the source work may have been recalled to the spectators' minds by association with the tune.

The first of the songs comes with the entry of Figaro in act I, scene 2. This is a piece composed specially for the play by Antoine Laurent Baudron (1742-1834). He joined the Comédie Française orchestra in 1763 and became its leader and conductor in 1766. The song shows us the lively character of Figaro, in the process of composing for the stage, associating himself with a hedonist philosophy. And yet, at the same time, it lays something of a false trail, since it associates the character with those traditional comic-servant qualities, intemperance and idleness which we shall find to be the very reverse of the character as we shall come to know him. Figaro's own running commentary is there to put us on our guard: 'ce qui

ne vaut pas la peine d'être dit...', 'quelque chose qui *eût l'air*
d'une pensée' (my italics). The full impact of the song is perhaps best understood in terms of the recurrent *game* which
Beaumarchais plays with his audience.

Ludic again is the framework into which Lindor's love-
song (I, 6) is integrated. It is probably the most attractively
scored pack of lies in French literature. This tune too was
composed by Baudron specially for the play. As it is presented
in the play, the song is supposed to be words of Lindor's
invention set, at Rosine's behest, to a familiar tune from a
recent work entitled *La Précaution inutile*. Rosine had dropped a copy of the original words from the casement, and of
course, *La Précaution inutile* is the subtitle of *Le Barbier*.
Although neither the words nor the tune are really quotations
from other works, the fact that it purports to be unoriginal
predisposes the audience to accepting the principle of the
integration of apposite quotation as the dramatic situation
demands it. In fact, all the musical episodes in *Le Barbier* are
justified by the plot or by psychology, and none is introduced
gratuitously.

Rosine's reply to Lindor's song, 'Tout me dit que Lindor
est charmant...' is the first actual quotation from another
work, and comes from *Le Maître en droit* (1760), an *opéra-
comique* by Monsigny, in which a doctor, hoping to marry his
pupil, Lise, loses her to the young lover, Lindor. Rosine sings
only the first two lines of Lise's ariette before the casement is
closed. But those of the audience who knew the full version
might deduce from it more about Rosine's attitude towards
her lover than it would have been acceptable to make explicit
on the stage of the Comédie Française at the time. The full
text of the song is this:

> Tout me dit que Lindor est charmant,
> Que je dois l'aimer constamment,
> Et que son cœur m'aime aussi tendrement.
> Oui, je me livre à ce doux espoir,
> Et, s'il était en mon pouvoir,
> Je voudrais moi-même hâter l'instant
> Où je dois le voir!

> Comment ne pas se rendre!
> Et comment se défendre
> De couronner ses feux,
> De combler ses vœux,
> Il a l'air si tendre!
> J'ai vu dans ses yeux
> D'un cœur amoureux
> Les transports heureux.
> Oui, je l'aimerai
> Tant que je vivrai.
> Ah! que ne peut-il m'entendre?

Of itself, this quotation is not enough to turn Rosine from an *innocente* into a *coquette,* but the vocabulary is fairly explicit and not totally out of tune with the Count's initially adulterous intentions towards her.

Before the explanations and *dénouement* of act IV, Rosine and Almaviva are on the stage together without Bartholo only in two very brief scenes (III, 6 and 9). As Roussin indicated (*28,* p. 387; see below), Beaumarchais contrived that in act III, scene 9, the vital message should not be transmitted. When Bartholo *is* present, as he nearly always is when the lovers are together, they either communicate in asides, or pass notes. Both methods emphasize difficulties of communication which totally preclude their talking together of love. Another way of circumventing these difficulties is to sing and, even when the words convey a false meaning, as in Lindor's song, the very fact of serenading Rosine – or singing to each other at all – is an indication of love.

Whereas Baudron's original songs (Figaro's 'Bannissons le chagrin...', Lindor's 'Vous l'ordonnez...' and Rosine's 'Quand, dans la plaine...') had the accompaniment of the full orchestra, consisting of a dozen or more players, Bartholo's *ritournelle* of act III, scene 5 ('Veux-tu, ma Rosinette...' – also by Baudron) was given only a minimal string accompaniment. Reminiscent of the *vaudevilles* of old *opéras-comiques,* this accompaniment would serve to underline its archaic flavour.

Vaudevilles, quoted sung snatches of popular or fashionable tunes, with their original words or with new ones, were included without special *dramatic* motivation in *opéras-co-*

miques, and were justified only by their appositeness. Whereas the technique of *vaudeville*-style quotation is used by Beaumarchais, the *fact* of singing is *vraisemblable* in his works whenever it occurs. It is *vraisemblable,* for instance, that the Count should sing to the tunes of currently known songs (II, 13). The impertinent satirical *signalement* of Bartholo would acquire enhanced impoliteness by being set – as it is generally held to have been – to the tune of the suggestive 'Ici sont venus en personne', which comes from a lost *opéra-comique,* composed before 1742 and entitled *Le Contrat de mariage* (see *27*). Similarly, the Count's hackneyed jokes about Bartholo's profession are appropriately set to music as the tipsy soldier becomes garrulous, uninhibited and overbearingly frank with the doctor. In performance, the first three lines (ll. 795-97) were probably pronounced rythmically with the tune in the background, before the Count actually broke into song for the last four lines. The point of quoting 'Vive le vin', which comes from Sedaine's *Le Déserteur,* is twofold. Firstly, it suggests a resemblance between the Count and Sedaine's Montauciel, a well-intentioned soldier with a fondness for drink, and, secondly, it recalls, albeit in broad terms, Montauciel's function, which is to look after the imprisoned *déserteur,* Alexis, who is under sentence of death. The parallel is possibly with the prisoner, Rosine, under sentence of marriage to Bartholo.

The last piece of music in the play is the storm music, played between acts III and IV. Like the other substantial pieces in the play, it was composed by Baudron, and its function is to suggest an atmosphere. Whereas all the quotations from other musical works have now lost their allusive capacity, this and Baudron's other compositions still embellish the performance (though, unfortunately, not the reading of the text) and still contribute to the attractiveness and liveliness which distinguish *Le Barbier* from the other plays which were being performed at the Comédie Française at the time. Although we may easily miss it nowadays, especially if we read rather than see this play, the music was acknowledged to be such an integral part of the play when it first appeared that the printers of the early editions pictured musical instruments in their textual ornaments.

5

Farce, Mimicry and Philosophy

'BEAUMARCHAIS fait flèche de tout bois'. This apposite
comment of Gabriel Conesa (*16*, p. 140) pinpoints one of the
most striking features of Beaumarchais's dramaturgy – its div-
ersity. We can examine the characterization, the structure and
the language of *Le Barbier* and still find aspects of the dramatic composition which deserve separate and more ample examination than such necessarily broad categories allow. Three
such aspects are farce, mimicry and philosophy. The final
version of the play is rich, for example, in the farcical elements
which recall its origin in the *intermède* and *parade* traditions
and enhance the liveliness of the play. It also contains several
aphoristic remarks, reminiscent of Enlightenment propaganda,
which give the play just a hint of seriousness.

Both the opening and closing acts are particularly redolent
of the farcical tradition. The polarizations of young versus old,
attractive versus ugly, noble versus commoner become evident
almost as soon as the curtain rises, for example, and the final
act sees both a lovers' quarrel and the defeat of the old tutor.
The outcome for Bartholo is typical of farce in that he is not
crushed but is obliged simply to accept, testily, that he is
the loser.

The alternation of the street and the balcony as focuses for
the action of act I mean that the Count and Figaro will slip
into hiding as Bartholo and Rosine appear (sc. 2, end), then
emerge as the casement closes (sc. 3-4), disappear just before
Bartholo comes out (sc. 4, end), re-emerge again (sc. 6), before
finally disappearing altogether (sc. 6, end). This repeated
movement has the 'mechanical' quality which is typical of
farce, conditioned as it is by the need for rapid and exact
timing in order for Figaro and Almaviva to avoid discovery.

In farce especially, attention to split-second timing is of para-
mount importance. This episode from act I also has the logic
of farce, since the most obvious subterfuge, though perfectly
understood by Bartholo, defies his capacity for coping with it.
Usually, the victim of a farcical stratagem does not understand
it, but, as Beaumarchais points out, Bartholo is more intelligent than most.

A. Roussin conducted an experiment with two actors in
order to illustrate Beaumarchais's handling of timing (*28,* pp.
387-90). From the beginning of the third act Almaviva needs
to tell Rosine that he has had to divulge her letter to Bartholo
in order to win his confidence. A short explanatory phrase,
such as 'J'ai dû montrer votre lettre à votre tuteur pour obtenir
sa confiance', is all that would be required. But, if this sentence
were said, much of the rest of the play would disappear. Beaumarchais therefore contrives to hold off this explanation until
act IV, scene 6. Roussin timed two actors playing act III, scene
4, lines 1166 to 1170 – the first opportunity for the Count to
tell Rosine what he had done – and proved that the crucial
sentence would take three seconds *less* to say than the five
sentences which cover those lines. And when the Count nearly
does manage to tell Rosine about the letter (III, 10, l. 1449)
the line needs to be interrupted by the returning Bartholo at
precisely the right moment to avoid a potentially disastrous
hiatus.

The structure of act IV is also clearly farcical. No sooner
does Bartholo leave by the door than the Count and Figaro
enter by the window. The marriage contract is hastily signed,
having been witnessed by the villain's venal accomplice, conveniently and instantaneously 'bought' for the purpose. Bartholo then arrives with the officers, an equally convenient
moment too late. By his vindictiveness in bringing the *alcade*
to ensure the arrest of the Count, he has stayed away too long
for his own interests and has thus contributed directly to his
own defeat. The villain scores a typically farcical own goal.
Once he arrives, he seizes as a *fripon* the one person on stage
who is innocent of any plotting – the notary. The whole process is finally validated according to the justice of farce, which
rules that the young lovers shall win the day, to the detriment

of the old guardian. Even the grounds of their triumph (as well as the process of it) are farcical: the youth, beauty and nobility of the lovers, and the assertion that an abuse of authority entails its forfeiture. No doubt this *ought* to be the case but, outside the world of the comic theatre, it is not *necessarily* the case.

The logic of farce operates equally in the action of acts II and III, where disguises and a simulated faint fool an otherwise perspicacious tutor, where eavesdropping and peeping from closets and exits via the back stairs are possible, and where anodyne letters can successfully be substituted for incriminating ones in the nick of time. And again, the doctor's humorously misnamed servants are prey to absurd yawning, sneezing and weeping which focuses our attention mainly on the vagaries of the rebellious and uncontrollable body while their master is trying to extract information from their minds. [12] Farcical characters in themselves, they serve to reinforce the farcical elements in the play, if one remembers that Bartholo will *always* be a prey to their incompetence. And yet it is ironical that, for all the exaggerated ridiculousness of their self-presentation, reason is in fact on their side in their dispute with Bartholo. What is against them is the traditional authority of the propertied classes.

One can also classify as farcical certain types of dialogue such as that in act III, scene 2 when Bartholo tells Alonzo to speak more loudly and then has to try to stop him bawling confidences at the top of his voice. [13] Or again, when, despite all the words which fly to and fro, it becomes obvious that

[12] The comment of the anonymous reader of *Le Barbier, opéra-comique,* on the scenes with the servants was 'clles tiennent un peu de la parade; n'est-ce pas un petit moyen de gaieté que La Jeunesse soit vieux et L'Eveillé imbécile?' (see *13,* p. 97). Medication to induce sneezing was consistent with the theory of the humours: 'toute exhalaison, d'après la théorie des humeurs, est un moyen naturel de faire disparaître du corps les humeurs mauvaises'. There was also a proverb: 'Quand le malade éternue, le médecin s'en retourne'. See F. Loux and P. Richard, *Sagesses du corps,* Paris, Maisonneuve et Larose, 1978, p. 92.

[13] Cf. the conversation between Toinette and Argan when she is introducing Cléante, disguised as a music teacher (*Le Malade imaginaire,* II, 2).

one character has quite failed to understand a situation which all the others, and the audience, *have* understood. Bazile throughout act III, scene 11 and the notary in act IV, scene 8 (ll. 1894-95) are cases in point. Again, the plot demands that the Count and Figaro should receive confirmation during act I of Bartholo's intention to marry Rosine. But to make Bartholo think aloud the sentence 'Il [Bazile] devait tout arranger pour que mon mariage se fît secrètement demain' (l. 328) is to make him divulge the very thing he should keep quiet. To follow that immediately by making his rival say 'Qu'ai-je entendu? Demain il épouse Rosine en secret!' (l. 330) is to display the artificiality of both dialogue and situation in the most visible way. In other words, Beaumarchais gets round the difficulty of how to confirm to the Count that the intentions of Bartholo are to be put into effect almost immediately, for which no subtle means is readily available, by using the most visibly unsubtle one. This has the two added advantages of appearing funny because it is both totally unlikely and shows the villain doing a disservice to himself, and of revealing to the audience the *mechanism,* and hence the manipulator.

Like many other plays, *Le Barbier* contains a lovers' quarrel (IV, 6). This is a situation common equally to high comedy and to farce, and is not more typical of one genre than of the other. Moreover, one cannot say categorically that such a quarrel derives its overall tone from the general tenor of the play in which it figures. (An analysis of *Tartuffe,* II, 4 and *Le Misanthrope,* IV, 3 would bear this out.) There are grounds for seeing the lovers' quarrel of *Le Barbier* as comedy rather than as farce. The stakes are high, despite our confidence that the misunderstanding will be resolved in the end. But more significant is the presentation of the scene, which is very reminiscent of the *drame.* This is particularly perceptible in the language which Rosine uses to the Count up to the point at which he reveals his true identity. Words such as *malheureux, profaner, dangereux, détester, t'abandonner au remords qui t'attend* are the stock in trade of the *drame,* which readily uses the most emphatic language to express acutely felt emotions. But this does not amount to proof. It could be argued instead that this manner of expression is sufficiently unusual in Rosine for us to be justified in feeling that the scene is being cast as a parody of the serious genre, and indeed the latter half of this scene (and the preceding scenes 4 and 5) could be interpreted as supporting such a reading.

Even discounting the elements of the *comedia dell'arte* and the *parades* which this play inherits, this would not be the only occasion on which *Le Barbier* mimicked other genres. It has been suggested that *l'infortunée Rosine* (ll. 215-16) and Bartholo's rhetorical lamentations over his broken shaving-kit (ll. 1440-42, 1450) are reminiscent of tragedy. Beaumarchais playfully suggested (2, p. 68, n. 2) that Bartholo may have composed a tragedy in his youth, and we have seen that *all* the characters compose in some way.

Mimicry, which Roger Caillois identifies as a basic form of play,[14] is not confined in *Le Barbier* to the imitation of other literary genres or of traditional and identifiable types (like the braggart soldier), which this play uses in a particular way (see below). Here, the characters not infrequently mimic each other. The variety of tones of the mimicry and the different shades of emotion which they reflect seem to indicate that mimicry itself is a fundamental element of Beaumarchais's dramaturgy. Figaro parodies Rosine's feigned dismay at dropping her song (ll. 186-88) by repeating some of her words exactly (ll. 217-18), and he follows the parody with a laugh and a general reflection about women. Both the parody and the reflection are intended to show an amused sympathy with Rosine. A modern spectator or reader may find this attitude, which pervades the play, rather patronizing, but that would not have been the reaction of the author's contemporaries. And the same sympathetic playfulness prompts Figaro to parody Almaviva's 'Que de grâces! que d'esprit!' (l. 389) with the syntactically and rhythmically identical 'Que de ruse! que d'amour!' (l. 390), underlining the suspicion that the Count is so entranced by Rosine's response that he is incapable of interpreting her behaviour objectively. In each case there is distancing between parodist and parodied, but the laughter is benign.

[14] *Les Jeux et les hommes*, Paris, Gallimard ('Idées'), 1958, chapter 2.

A quite differently motivated style of mimicry comes from Bartholo when he parodies La Jeunesse's sneezing (l. 605). Bartholo's power to control the situation is severely curtailed by his servant's incapacity, and the parody signifies an exasperation verging on contempt. As spectators and readers, we, of course, laugh both at the exasperation and at its source. Another example of Bartholo's mimicry is more subtle. In lines 742-43 he reproduces more or less exactly Rosine's thoughts of act II, scene 1. Only the audience is in a position to see it as mimicry (Rosine would see it as astuteness) because only the spectators will realize its exactness. By being based on the shrewdness of the doctor's guesswork, it underlines the disparity of power which separates the two characters. In a context where the final outcome was less of a foregone conclusion, this type of mimicry would be more disturbing, because it consists in making a game of an opponent's efforts to master a situation.

At the hands of Figaro, Bartholo himself becomes an object of mimicry in act III, scene 5. Inspired by Rosine's singing in act III, scene 4, Bartholo adapts a song to his own situation and accompanies it with a burlesque dance, which Figaro parodies behind his back. (Whether Bartholo catches sight of Figaro's action or not is not clear from the text.) A grotesque parody of a grotesque original, Figaro's mimicry underlines the distance in age, social competence, attractiveness and so on which separates the two sides in the contest. Like Bartholo's imitation of La Jeunesse, its aim is to belittle its object by emphasizing his physical shortcomings, as well – in this case – as the lack of self-awareness which allows him to display them.

I suggested earlier that the Figaro-Almaviva partnership could be seen as a kind of composite hero figure in which the attributes of one character complemented the other's. This composite may well have been how the talented, renamed and newly noble Beaumarchais saw himself. But if we look at the activities of Almaviva in the play, we see that he is himself painted as a composite figure. For most of the play, the nobleman appears in a plebeian disguise, or rather, in three: the *abbé,* the soldier, the student teacher of music. And, even in act IV, the marks identifying his caste are covered for most of the time by a *large manteau*. The noble is therefore borrowing a plebeian identity and all the freedom of movement which this brings with it. He is, as he explains in act I, scene 1, disguised in order to escape from himself *qua* dissolute court noble. And yet, the disguise is put on, like a carnival costume, with its overtones of ambiguity and sexual adventure, to facilitate an amorous escapade which is merely transmuted, for the sake of the theatrical propriety of the Comédie Française, into a quest for a wife. Once the objective is achieved, and only then, disguises are cast off, and, in a flash, Almaviva flings off his cloak to reveal his real identity. Seldom has such an indelicate theme been so decorously treated.

But in the theatre – and from time to time Beaumarchais, as we have seen, reminds us that that is precisely where we are – the characters on stage are *already* disguised. The play is a game of mimicry, and the theatre is an institutionalized form of mimicry. So too is the carnival. Theatre, carnival, masked ball, *le travesti* were prominent elements in the leisure activities of the court nobility of the seventeenth and eighteenth centuries. Moreover, the personal disguise tended often enough towards the plebeian, even while the setting remained noble. Marie-Antoinette and her ladies, dressed as dairymaids, occupying themselves in the Queen's Dairy at Rambouillet (built in 1785-86) is a particularly interesting example of this in that the 'rusticated' noblewomen play in an elegant neoclassical marble dairy with its annexed grotto of carefully counterfeited 'natural' rock formations. Is the notable preoccupation of this society (Beaumarchais's adopted sphere) with plebeian disguise more than just a sentimental idealization of country life? Institutionalized into acceptability, like the theatre and the carnival, by being delimited in time and space, does it perhaps mirror the nobles' half-acknowledged feelings of fascination with or even envy of the commoners and the *insouciance* one half-believed they enjoyed? And might it be evidence of nostalgia for the protection of the dimly remembered and hence idealized simplicity and innocence of childhood occupations?

It is in no way surprising that Beaumarchais, as a representative of his age and its culture, should reflect this preoccupation with disguise and transformation in his life and works. Roger Caillois (op. cit., pp. 162, 166) points to the interdependence of games and cultures, and he observes that games, which are both components and reflections of cultures at given points in their evolution, express, inevitably even if imprecisely, a culture's general nature, with its inherent values and weaknesses. If Caillois is right, institutionalized leisure activities based on a fantasized mobility between the social strata are of particular significance in France in the closing years of the Ancien Régime.

And might the feelings which I referred to above be experienced with particular acuteness by Beaumarchais, who so successfully rose in society – as he was indeed reminded from time to time? And would this perhaps account for the dramatic construction, which reverses reality, whereby Almaviva-Beaumarchais wears the plumage of the ugly duckling for most of the time, in order to reveal his true identity as the swan at the moment of triumph? Might Beaumarchais be affirming that *he* is really a swan, despite any appearances to the contrary?

We can go further. Clément Borgal referred to the philosophical commonplaces and Enlightenment punchlines which Beaumarchais incorporated into his works as *miettes philosophiques,* and that is precisely how they come across – as *miettes.* The writer warns us against considering them out of context (see especially *15,* pp. 81-82 and 93-94). If one does isolate them in this way, one can build up a picture of Beaumarchais the revolutionary, the subverter of the Ancien Régime – a picture which is perfectly ridiculous, given that he was quite at home within the system and played it with notable skill. But if one considers the philosophical statements within the context of a play which both gives expression to the *déclassé* writer's psychical dilemma and which constantly directs the spectator's attention on to the presence of the author himself, then their function becomes clear. They advertise Beaumarchais as being a modern, progressive thinker, while their triteness and fragmented presentation – for the 'crumbs'

do not coalesce into a sustained and comprehensive philoso-
phico-political position – keep them, in *Le Barbier* at least,
within the limits of political acceptability. Thus the supporter
of the Ancien Régime can enjoy some of the benefits of the
system while at the same time assuming the mantle of its critic,
and hence enjoy also the popularity which such a stance
brought him. Certainly, this interpretation of evidence from
Le Barbier is supported by Beaumarchais's conduct in the
Goëzman affair.

In his article on Beaumarchais's philosophical and moral
thinking, R. Navarri shows how the author articulated his
philosophy of life through Figaro, whose idea of his *intérêt*
leads him to pilot his way towards personal fulfilment through
a selfish and anarchical society composed of individuals whose
conduct justifies his own. This explains why such stress is
laid on Figaro's courage and dynamism. But, if Beaumarchais
shares this outlook with other members of an active and politi-
cally ambitious bourgeoisie, he does not underestimate the part
played by Chance in human affairs, and his optimism is tinged
with an element of fatalism which runs directly counter to his
belief in the value of individual effort – a belief which can only
ever be validated and sustained when one's undertakings are
marked by success. Navarri argues that Beaumarchais, like
d'Holbach, Diderot and, especially, Helvétius, denies the existence of absolute moral principles and hence shares with them
an opposition to a feudal social structure and to its theological
justifications. 'Pour lui comme pour eux', Navarri writes, 'le
mobile essentiel de tout acte réside dans la sensibilité, la passion et d'une manière plus générale dans l'intérêt, le profit,
dont l'homme poursuit la réalisation conformément à sa nature'
(*23*, p. 139) – a fundamentally bourgeois position. In *Le Barbier* at least, where 'punir un fripon en se rendant heureux' is
the aim of the protagonists, no conflict is envisaged between
the self-interest of the individual and the interest of society
as a whole. Nonetheless, the determination with which Figaro
pursues the Count's interests, which he has made his own,
clearly shows that such a conflict is always latent, and is only
kept at the latent level by the invocation of a 'virtuous', socially desirable purpose – the releasing of Rosine from Bartholo's

unjust tutelage. Beaumarchais's ethical stance in the Figaro comedies remains, however, ambiguous. Figaro's main preoccupation is with success at all costs, and challenging the social and political system takes second place to it. In this, Figaro mirrors his creator. But it is Beaumarchais's awareness of the inevitable precariousness of his own social position, which depends on playing the system with sufficient skill to profit from it and not be crushed by its arbitrariness and injustice, that provides the stimulus for his albeit unadventurous, philosophical protests against its abuses.

Le Barbier has a traditional plot, structured round a series of expedients and reversals and animated by characters whose existence we amuse ourselves by believing in for an hour and a half. It makes a sophisticated use of a wide range of linguistic resources and includes musical elements both witty and attractive, as well as others derived from the author's personal experience and philosophy of life. If, as Pierre Voltz argues, the history of comedy is the history of individual cases (*32*, p. 8), this play, like *Le Mariage* which was to follow it, is an outstanding example of a comedy which draws on a long and varied theatrical tradition without ever giving the impression of being merely derivative. It provokes by turns a whole range of reactions in the spectator, including broad laughter, smiles, sympathy, charm, intellectual assent and disagreement, revulsion, surprise and emotional satisfaction. If it is somewhat overshadowed by *Le Mariage,* its qualities too have inspired composers, most notably Rossini, and time has shown it to be one of the undisputed landmarks of European drama.

Select Bibliography

M A N Y useful studies of Beaumarchais and his works have appeared over the years. The list below is confined strictly to the most recent, accessible and generally useful to undergraduates studying *Le Barbier*. Works cited incidentally are described in the footnotes. Attention is drawn to the following work: *Beaumarchais: a bibliography,* by Brian N. Morton and Donald C. Spinelli, Ann Arbor, The Olivia and Hill Press, Inc., 1988.

EDITIONS

1. *Le Barbier de Séville,* edited by E. J. Arnould, Oxford, Blackwell, 1963.
2. *Le Barbier de Séville,* edited by G. Bonneville, Paris, Bordas, 1976 (reprinted 1981).
3. *Le Barbier de Séville,* preface by M. Etcheverry, commentaries and notes by G. Conesa, Paris, Livre de Poche, 1985.
4. *Le Barbier de Séville,* edited by L. Lejealle, Paris, Larousse, 1970.
5. *Le Barbier de Séville,* with *Jean-Bête à la Foire,* edited by J. Scherer, Paris, Gallimard (Folio), 1982.
6. *Mémoires de Beaumarchais dans l'affaire Goëzman,* Paris, Garnier, 1873.
7. *Notes et réflexions,* with an introduction by G. Bauer, Paris, Hachette, 1961.
8. *Parades,* edited by P. Larthomas, Paris, SEDES, 1977.
9. *Œuvres,* edited by P. Larthomas, Paris, NRF-Gallimard (Bibliothèque de la Pléiade), 1988.
10. *Théâtre,* edited by J.-P. de Beaumarchais, Paris, Garnier, 1980.
11. *Théâtre,* edited by R. Pomeau, Paris, Garnier-Flammarion, 1965.

CRITICAL STUDIES

12. Arnould, E. J., '*Le Barbier de Séville* et la critique', *French Studies,* XVI, 4 (October 1962), pp. 334-47.

13.   Arnould, E. J., *La Genèse du Barbier de Séville,* Dublin, The University Press and Paris, Minard, 1965.

14.   Beaumarchais, J.-P. de, 'Un Inédit de Beaumarchais: *Le Sacristain',* *Revue d'Histoire littéraire de la France,* 74, 6 (November-December 1974), pp. 976-99.

15.   Borgal, C., *Beaumarchais,* Paris, Editions Universitaires (Classiques du XXe siècle, 115), 1972.

16.   Conesa, G., *La Trilogie de Beaumarchais: écriture et dramaturgie,* Paris, Presses Universitaires de France (Littératures Modernes), 1985.

17.   Coulet, H., 'La Notion de caractère dans l'œuvre de Beaumarchais', *Revue de l'Université de Moncton,* XI, 3 (1978), pp. 21-32.

18.   Dauvin, S. and J., *Beaumarchais: Le Barbier de Séville,* Paris, Hatier (Profil d'une œuvre), 1981.

19.   Descotes, M., *Les Grands Rôles du théâtre de Beaumarchais,* Paris, Presses Universitaires de France, 1974.

20.   Emelina, J., *Les Valets et les servantes dans le théâtre comique en France de 1610 à 1700,* Grenoble, Presses Universitaires de Grenoble, 1975.

21.   *Europe,* 528 (April 1973): *Beaumarchais.*

22.   Larthomas, P., 'Le Style de Beaumarchais dans *Le Barbier de Séville* et *Le Mariage de Figaro', Information littéraire,* 23 (1981), pp. 54-56.

23.   Navarri, R., 'Réflexions sur quelques aspects de la pensée philosophique et morale de Beaumarchais', *La Pensée,* 110 (July-August 1963), pp. 136-41.

24.   Pomeau, R., '*Le Barbier de Séville*: de l'intermède à la comédie', *Revue d'Histoire littéraire de la France,* 74, 6 (November-December 1974), pp. 963-75.

25.   ———, *Beaumarchais,* Paris, Hatier (Connaissance des Lettres, 47), 1962.

26.   ———, *Beaumarchais; ou la bizarre destinée,* Paris, Presses Universitaires de France (Ecrivains), 1987.

27.   Robinson, P., *La Musique des comédies de Figaro: éléments de dramaturgie,* in *Studies on Voltaire and the Eighteenth Century,* vol. 275 (Oxford, The Voltaire Foundation, 1990), pp. 359-499.

28.   Roussin, A., 'Les Grandes Premières: *Le Barbier de Séville', Conferencia,* 15 September 1950, pp. 374-90.

29.   Sanaker, J. K., 'Le Figaro de Beaumarchais, le valet embourgeoisé', in *Actes du 8e congrès des romanistes scandinaves; études romanes de l'Université d'Odense,* 13, Odense University Press, 1983, pp. 293-301.

30.   Scherer, J., *La Dramaturgie de Beaumarchais,* Paris, Nizet, 3rd edition, 1980.

31.   Van Tieghem, P., *Beaumarchais par lui-même,* Paris, Editions du Seuil (Ecrivains de Toujours), 1960.

32.   Voltz, P., *La Comédie,* Paris, A. Colin (Collection U), 1964.